Young Readers Edition

THE DESERT

A. Starker Leopold

and the Editors of Time-Life Books

TIME INCORPORATED NEW YORK

ON THE COVER: Cow-blinder cactus, a kind of prickly pear that grows in the desert, has paddle-shaped joints covered with tiny, sharp spines.

LIFE WORLD LIBRARY

LIFE NATURE LIBRARY

TIME READING PROGRAM

THE LIFE HISTORY OF THE UNITED STATES

LIFE SCIENCE LIBRARY

GREAT AGES OF MAN

TIME-LIFE LIBRARY OF ART

TIME-LIFE LIBRARY OF AMERICA

FOODS OF THE WORLD

THIS FABULOUS CENTURY

LIFE LIBRARY OF PHOTOGRAPHY

© 1967, 1970 Time Inc. All rights reserved.
Published simultaneously in Canada.
Library of Congress catalogue card number 67-29089.

Contents

1 Scorched Belts of the Earth — 7

2 Water—the Eternal Problem — 27

3 Plant Life on the Arid Land — 35

4 The World of Desert Animals — 51

5 Staying Alive in the Desert — 71

6 Man against the Desert — 85

7 Taming the Desert for Mankind's Use — 111

Index — 126
For Further Reading — 128
Credits and Acknowledgments — 128

Introduction

Stretches of lonely sand dunes, dry lakes, distant rock formations shimmering in the heat—this is what most people picture when they think of the desert. Thus it seems fitting that the word "desert" comes from a Latin word meaning "abandoned." In reality the deserts are anything but abandoned. All of them contain plants, animals and even humans, as well as some of the world's most inspiring scenery.

During the past 25 years there has been a tremendous increase in man's interest in the arid lands. Biological, physical and social scientists are investigating many broad problems common to all deserts. These range from questions as general as our "fossil" ground water, which may be 25,000 years old, to the water balance in tiny desert kangaroo mice, which have already solved the problem of living without drinking water.

The desert is man's future land bank. Fortunately, it is a large reserve offering eight million square miles of space for human occupation. It is also, fortunately, a rich bank, which may turn green when man uses desalted sea water for irrigation.

When this happens it will surely be one of the greatest transformations made by man in his constant and successful role in changing the face of the planet. Indeed, an end result of this activity could be, to many, a far less fascinating world to live in—a completely domesticated earth.

CHARLES H. LOWE JR.
Professor of Zoology
The University of Arizona

ROCK FORMATIONS in Utah's Bryce Canyon, resembling ancient ruins, are all that remain of a once-massive limestone plateau. Uncounted centuries of activity by vanished rivers, which gouged away soft stone, and by desert winds, which scour the remaining rock, have left these lonely spires.

1
Scorched Belts of the Earth

To most people, the word desert brings to mind a wasteland of sand—scorched by the sun and scoured by the wind, waterless and empty of shelter; lifeless except for poisonous creatures lurking under rocks. Few people venture into the desert or even want to.

Yet, for those who know it, the desert is a fascinating and very beautiful place. Its harsh setting is the home of an amazing

Deserts: Where and Why

The world's deserts and the main forces that produce them are shown on the map at right. Most deserts lie within belts of land fairly close to the Tropic of Cancer and the Tropic of Capricorn. In these areas, the winds are very dry. Deserts on the coast are swept by onshore breezes that have been chilled by cold ocean currents and can carry only a little water as they move inland; by the time these winds reach inland deserts or those lying behind mountains, most of their moisture is gone.

DESERTS

DRYING WINDS

COLD OCEAN CURRENTS

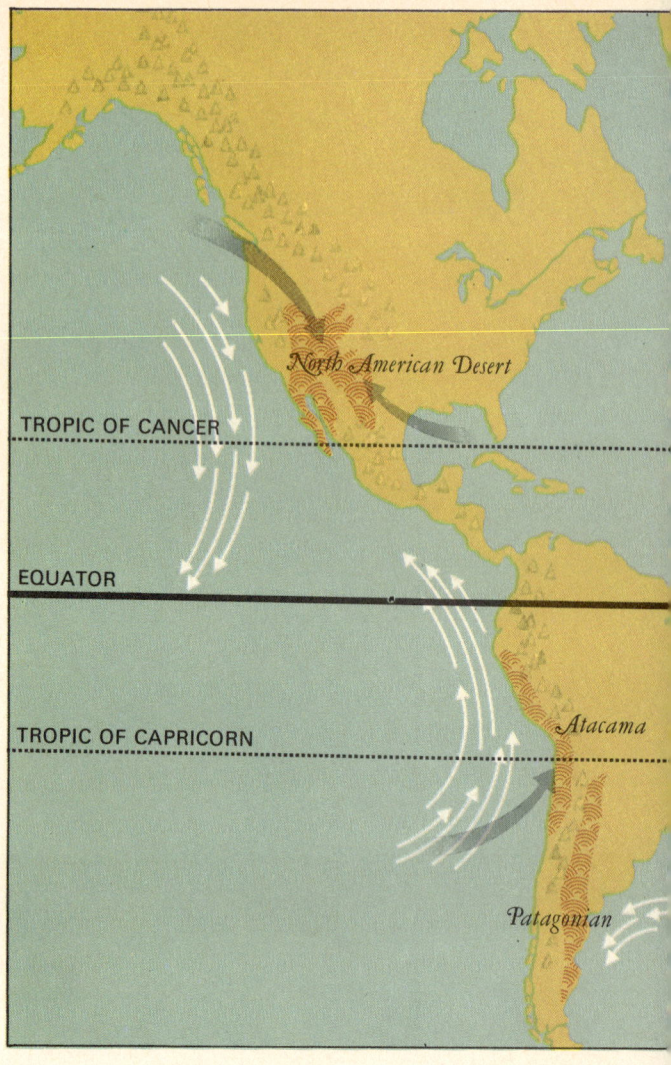

variety of animals and plants that have developed the ability to thrive under conditions of extreme heat and dryness. Since the ground is not hidden by a cover of plants, as it is in other climates, the landscape displays some of the earth's most spectacular natural forms. After a rare rain, the splendor of desert flowers in bloom rivals that of any tropical garden.

Scientists have defined the conditions that must exist before an area can be called a desert; there must be generally high temperatures and less than 10 inches of rainfall a year for land to fall into this classification. The biggest desert of all is the Sahara, which stretches across the whole 3,200-mile width of North Africa and occupies nearly a third of the entire continent. The Sahara is almost as big as the entire United States, including Hawaii and Alaska.

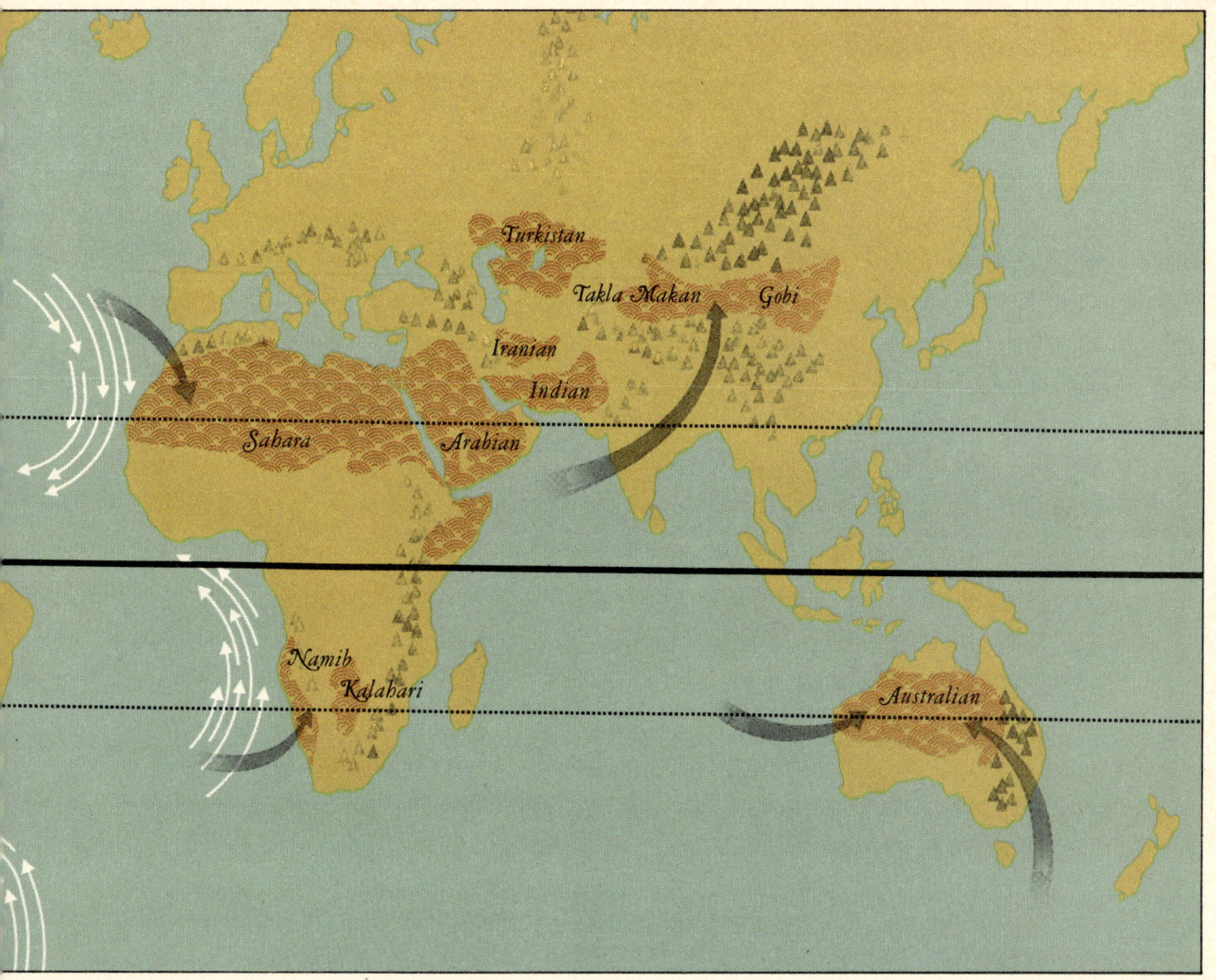

In the Southern Hemisphere is the Australian Desert, which occupies 44 per cent of the continent compared to 5 per cent for the deserts of North America. With an average of five inches of rain a year in its driest places, the 1.3-million-square-mile Australian Desert is not as dry as the Sahara.

The Arabian Desert spreads over nearly a million square miles of the Arabian peninsula. About a third of this is covered with sand, a greater fraction than in any other desert. It has another distinction, a complete absence of permanent rivers. There are no watered mountains to act as river sources.

The Turkistan, a desert of three quarters of a million square miles in southwest Russia, is dwarfed by the vast and more productive steppes adjoining it. Here, where man has struggled against aridity through centuries of turbulent history, agriculture

Ovenlike Days

The desert is fiercely hot in daytime because it is rarely covered by moisture-filled clouds, which can deflect the sun's rays. Therefore, 90 per cent of the rays reaching the earth heat the ground. In better-watered regions, only 40 per cent of the sun's radiation reaches the earth.

remains minor. The desert's western border is the Caspian Sea, which almost went dry 6,000 years ago and was refilled when the Near East began to get more rainfall in the 2,000 years before the Christian Era. Today, looking down through 10 feet of water, we can see the foundations of a community built on the Caspian's shores in drier prehistoric times.

The North American desert has within it nearly 500,000 square miles of strange, varied land in the Southwestern United States and northwestern part of Mexico. The desert has four major divisions: the Great Basin, Mojave, Sonoran and Chihuahuan Deserts.

Most of the Great Basin Desert, named for the basin between the Rockies and the Sierra Nevada-Cascade Ranges, is steppe or semidesert. In southern Nevada and western Utah it becomes a true desert, merging gradually with the Mojave of southeastern California. The Mojave is actually a small transitional area between the Great Basin and the Sonoran Desert to the south. The Sonoran is the desert most familiar to Americans, stretching from southeast California across southern Arizona into the southwest corner of New Mexico, and onward into So-

10

Iceboxlike Nights

Nights on the desert are often intensely cold. The lack of cloud cover that causes high daytime temperatures (*opposite*) also allows 90 per cent of the day's accumulated heat to escape. In humid regions, the earth retains about half of the day's heat, thus creating warmer nights.

nora and Baja California in Mexico. The Chihuahuan lies to the east of the great Sierra Madre Occidental, spreading north into southwest Texas, southern New Mexico and the southeast corner of Arizona.

The Patagonian Desert (260,000 square miles) of Argentina has a place name too well established for it to be changed, but most of the true Argentine desert, as opposed to grassland, occurs to the north in what is called the Monte.

The Thar (230,000 square miles) in western India and Pakistan, also known as the Great Indian Desert, lies to the east of the Indus River. The wet air flow of the summer monsoon passes nearby, to the east, without dropping rain on the Thar. The Indus Valley was the home of thriving civilizations 4,000 to 5,000 years ago. Cities like Mohenjo-Daro and Harappa had oversized street drains and baths in most houses, and it is quite possible that the Indus Valley shared the monsoon downpours at that time and declined into a desert after a shift in the wind direction.

The Kalahari in southern Africa covers 220,000 arid square miles with a much great-

Abstract Art on a Desert Floor

The combined actions of wind, sun and rare rainfall can produce spectacular patterns in a desert. The aerial view of the Libyan Desert (*right*) shows huge dunes formed by winds that blow smaller dunes together. These dunes, several hundred feet high, stretch for miles. In the photo below, a drying mud flat cracks only hours after a rain; the moisture has either evaporated or seeped far underground.

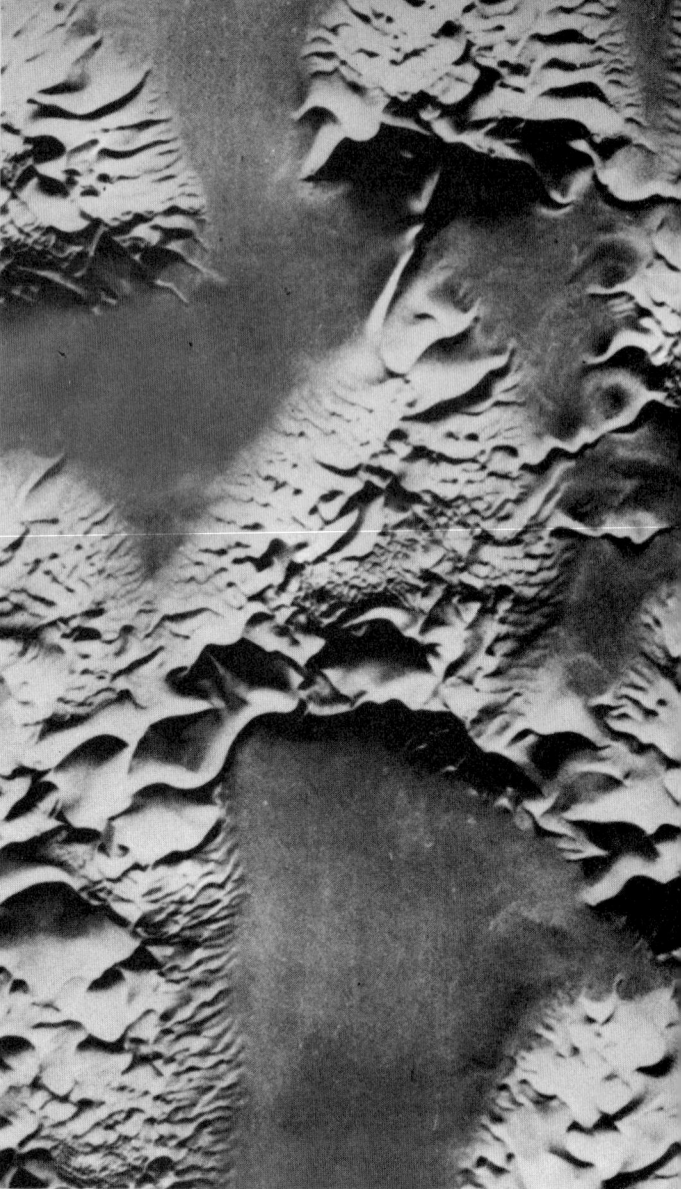

er area of dry grassland blending into it.

The Takla Makan (200,000 square miles) in Sinkiang Province of western China is landlocked, far from any moisture source. It merges with great semiarid regions to the northwest and in Mongolia, the location of the famed Gobi, a barren grassland steppe.

The Iranian (150,000 square miles) of old Persia is small as true deserts go, yet it boasts some of the world's highest sand dunes, over 700 feet in height. In and near this desert are many traces of Neolithic men, the world's first agriculturalists, as well as the ruins of later, powerful empires. The evidence for any recent climatic change here is not final, but there are signs in Iran and elsewhere in the Middle East that man's misuse of land has ruined fertile areas and turned them to deserts.

The Atacama-Peruvian in Chile and Peru is, with 140,000 square miles, the smallest desert of all and has the least precipitation—

less than half an inch a year on the average. The coastal edge of the desert is extremely foggy. Even though the moisture does not condense as rain, plants and animals manage to use some of it.

Deserts are full of surprises, as the largest, the Sahara, shows. While the Sahara is known for gigantic sand dunes, these make up only about one tenth of its area. It has mountains 11,500 feet high—so tall that they have snow on their peaks. And even though annual rainfall in the interior averages only one inch, the Sahara contains a lake as big as the State of New Jersey. To people who live in temperate lands, the most unexpected fact about the Sahara is that it is home for more than three million people.

The major feature of all deserts is, of course, dryness. There are places in Mexico's Baja California peninsula that receive no rain at all for four or five years in a row; one especially unfortunate location in the Sahara

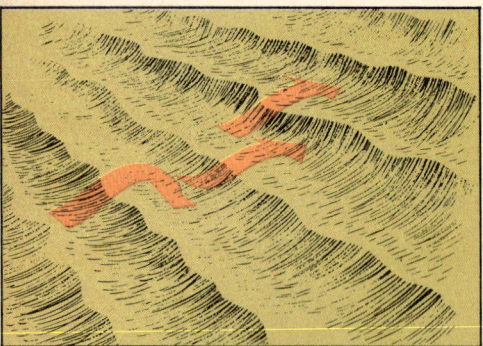
TRANSVERSE DUNES

BARKHAN DUNES

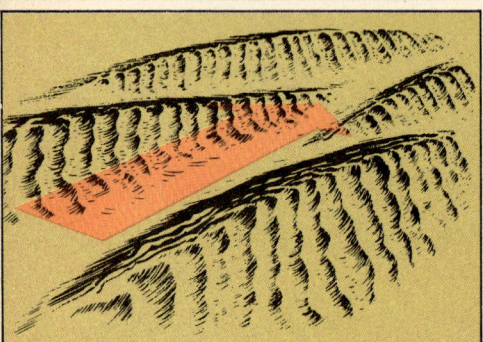
LONGITUDINAL DUNES

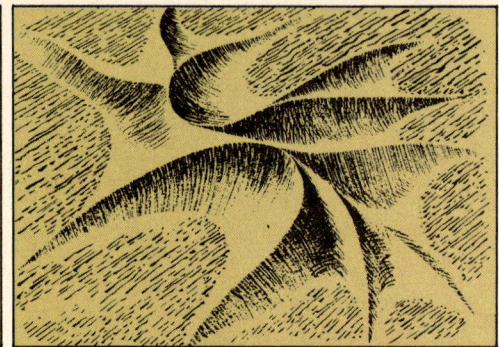
STAR DUNES

The Many Shapes of Wind-Blown Sand

The caravan seen at right is avoiding the soft sands of a cluster of dunes. Transverse, barkhan and longitudinal dunes form where winds come from one direction. Transverses are produced by moderate winds (*arrows*) that carry the finer sand grains away while leaving ridges composed of coarser particles. Barkhans occur where sand is relatively scarce; the wind forms crescents since it can blow more easily along the dunes' lower tips than over the higher centers. Longitudinals result when strong winds (*arrow*) move both fine and coarse grains and cut deep troughs through the waves of sand. Star dunes are formed in areas where winds blow from all directions. Of the dunes shown here, only star dunes remain stationary for any long periods of time.

once went without any rain for 11 years.

As well as being dry, deserts are among the hottest places in the world. The highest air temperature ever recorded on earth— 136.4° F. in the shade—was measured in Azizia, in the Libyan part of the Sahara. Summer temperatures of 120° are common in many deserts and, during the day, the surface of the ground absorbs so much heat that it is often 30° to 50° hotter than the air.

The reason for these high temperatures is the desert's dryness. In temperate climates, moisture in the air forms an insulating blanket that shields the earth's surface from some of the sun's scorching rays. The lack of this insulation causes the desert to heat up rapid-

The Erosive Carvings of Water

Carrying sharp fragments of gravel and stone, the Colorado River rushes through a Utah canyon. The rough sediment in this water has amazing cutting powers; in the past million years, this river has carved a snakelike path deep into the earth.

ly during the day and to cool off rapidly at night *(pages 10 and 11)*. Often the difference between the day's high and the night's low can be as much as 50°.

Like its climate, the soil of the desert is quite different from that of more temperate regions. Because there is little rain, minerals do not get washed out of the soil as they do in wetter parts of the world. Depending on which minerals are present, desert soil can be extremely fertile or nearly barren. The salt flats in Utah, for instance, are too salty to support plant life, but their trapped minerals —especially potash, which is used as a fertilizer—are a profitable mining resource. In California's Imperial Valley, on the other hand, mineral deposits make the soil among the most fertile in the United States—though, of course, it must be watered by irrigation.

Besides improving soil fertility, the desert's minerals can even improve the nutritional value of the crops grown there. Some of the best alfalfa hay in North America comes from desert fields in Nevada that are irrigated with water from the Humboldt River. The hay sells at premium prices and is fed to race horses and herds of fine cattle.

For those who have never studied deserts, it comes as a shock to discover that they cover a seventh of the globe—eight million square miles. Most of this land is located in two broad belts, one on each side of the equator *(pages 8 and 9)*, that get little rain from the movement of air over the earth.

The spinning of the earth, which is fastest

Cycle of Wear

These diagrams show, in simplified form, how deserts are shaped by millions of years of erosion. In early stages, swift streams carve channels in a newly formed plateau. As time passes, the mature channels have been widened, isolating canyons, buttes and mountains from the plateau. In the old phase, the buttes and mountains are almost gone, and the valleys have filled with sediment to form a plain.

THE YOUNG LANDSCAPE

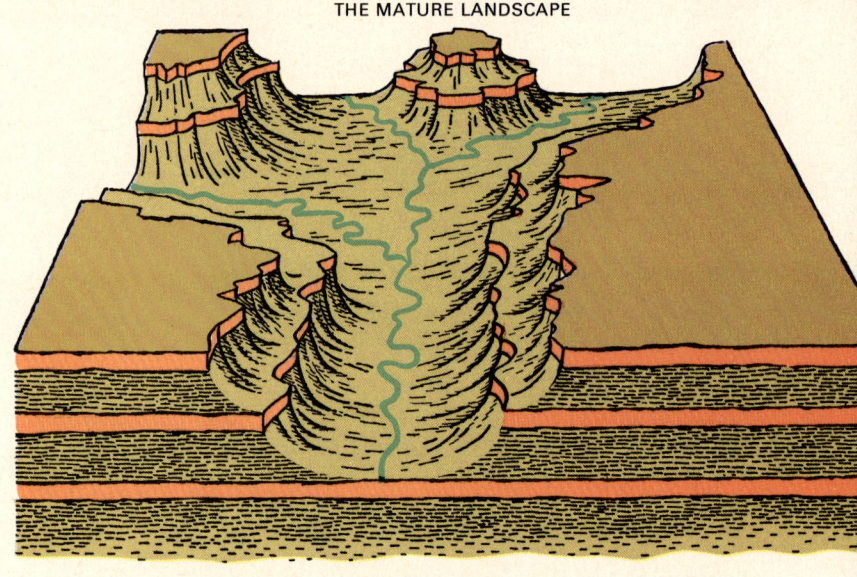

THE MATURE LANDSCAPE

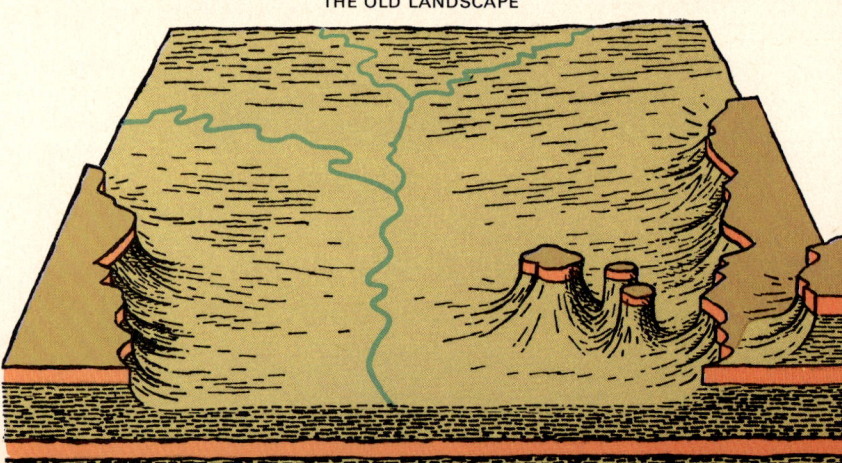

THE OLD LANDSCAPE

at the equator and slowest at the poles, causes air masses to move up and down in more-or-less permanent patterns. Over the equator, the spinning motion thrusts the air upward, where it is cooled and drops its water in the form of rain. Thus the equatorial region is generally wet. But on either side of this region the air currents move down again toward the earth. The air warms as it moves down, picking up water and thus drying out the earth underneath. The two belts of land under the downward-moving air currents are the most common locations for deserts.

The spinning earth sets up currents in the oceans as well as in the atmosphere, and movements of the waters also play a part in the formation of deserts. Cold ocean currents from the poles flow toward the equator. Winds blowing over these cold currents are cooled so that they drop their water. Later, when they pass over the land, these winds are warmed, pick up any available ground moisture and keep tne land dry. A desert that was formed this way is located along the coast of Peru, where the prevailing westerly winds blow across the cold Peru Current onto the land.

Geography too contributes to the formation of deserts. Some places are simply too far from the ocean, the primary source of moisture. Winds reaching the Gobi, deep inside Asia, and the interior of the Sahara have traveled over such vast expanses of land that the air has been squeezed dry of water before it reaches these deserts.

Places close to an ocean can also be deserts if they are separated from the coast by a mountain range. This is because the wet ocean air is cooled as it is forced upward to clear the peaks, and loses its water in the form of rain. Thus, there is little or no moisture left to be dropped on the far side of the mountains. In addition, as the air starts moving downward again, on the other side of the mountains, it warms and sucks up what little water the already-dry land has. This process is strikingly evident on the West Coast of the United States. Winds blowing off the Pacific Ocean drop rain on the western slopes of the Cascade-Sierra Nevada Mountains and dry out the eastern slopes into a desert. Mountains are such efficient water traps that some of the world's driest and wettest places are located next to each other, separated only by a mountain wall.

Compared to vast ocean currents and huge mountains, the role of man in the creation of deserts may not seem like much. But he often plays an important part. Many regions of the world with light rainfall are kept from becoming real deserts by a light covering of sparse vegetation. These plants protect the soil from drying out under the fierce attacks of wind and sun. The plants' roots also help to hold the soil and prevent it from being washed or blown away.

All too often, however, man has disturbed this delicate balance. He has allowed his herds of animals to overgraze and kill off the

(Text continued on page 22)

Toward a Greener Desert: The Art of Redistributing Water

This imaginary landscape shows typical desert land forms and several methods man uses to turn sand into productive soil. This desert is dry because winds generally lose their moisture in the form of rain or snow on the seaward side of the mountains. A few snow-fed streams plunge down, carrying away rocks

and earth in their path to form canyons; as they slow, some streams drop their silt to make alluvial fans, and others end in salty lakes surrounded by salt flats. Mesas and buttes are columns of rock left after softer formations are eroded by wind, water and sand. Some underground water reaches the desert surface along faults (cracks in subsurface rock) that tap water-bearing layers to form seepage wells and oases. Man supplies most of the water to reclaim the desert by drilling artesian wells through waterproof layers, damming streams, building pumping stations and pipelines and, sometimes, desalting ocean water.

(1) CULTIVATION

(2) OVERCULTIVATION

(3) GRAZING

How Man Can Make a Desert

When man begins cultivating dry, virgin land *(1)*, he starts destroying the plant roots that hold soil and prevent erosion. If he should overcultivate the flatland, he often plants up the hill *(2)*, baring more land to wind and water. When the land no longer supports crops, man may use it for grazing *(3)*, which accelerates erosion. As grasses disappear, he turns the slopes over to goats and sheep *(4)*, which strip it of the remaining green. The desolation *(5)* is then complete: the land is dusty and barren—a desert.

protective plants *(above and opposite)*. He has also plowed up the natural covering of vegetation in order to plant crops. Many areas of the Middle East where agriculture flourished have been turned into real deserts in this way. And the same thing happened during the 1930s when parts of the Southwestern United States were improperly farmed. Millions of tons of topsoil were carried hundreds of miles away by the wind, and the area became what is still called the "Dust Bowl."

Once formed, deserts go through three distinct steps of aging as the land is worn down by erosion. There are young deserts, middle-aged deserts and old deserts *(page 18)*. Oddly enough though drought creates deserts, it is water that shapes them. Though rare, desert storms are usually sudden and furious. When they do come, they often come in excess, dumping several years' worth of water in one huge downfall. Because the dry

(4) BARREN GROUND

(5) DESOLATION

ground has been baked so hard, it cannot even soak up the water when it finally arrives. Flash floods hurtle down barren gullies, and the floodwater carries with it vast quantities of sand, stones and sometimes even boulders. These are the "tools" of erosion. They cut and batter at the land, shaping the desert into wonderfully varied forms.

Many of these strange forms owe their shapes to the fact that all parts of a desert do not wear away at the same rate, and softer material, of course, erodes more rapidly than harder material. Thus in some deserts, particularly in the Southwestern United States, there are large, flat-topped hills called mesas ("tables" in Spanish) that rear above the desert floor. These hills, whose flat tops are made of very hard, protective stone, were left standing while the area around them was worn away.

But in time, even a hard-surfaced mesa will wear away and become a smaller, steep-sided hill known as a butte. And buttes may themselves erode after many centuries, leaving nothing more than some tall, chimney-like columns of rock to mark the location of what once was probably a huge plateau.

Water is not the only erosive force that wears deserts away. Wind, too, does its part —though it is not quite as effective as water. Like water, wind also uses a "tool" to erode the landscape: sand.

Sand is comparatively heavy, and even a strong wind can rarely lift it more than a few feet off the ground. The result is that rocks eroded by wind-driven sand are often top-heavy, because the sand has chewed away their bases. In this same way, unprotected telephone poles are simply sawed off at the bottom by blowing sand. Even metal shields placed around their bases are unable to pro-

23

tect these poles for more than a few years.

Blowing sand creates dunes, among the most spectacular of desert landforms, which sometimes reach 700 feet in height and stretch six times as long. As immobile as they appear, some sand dunes actually move over the desert floor. According to the direction in which wind blows, dunes can take different shapes. In areas where sand is relatively scarce and the wind blows steadily in one direction, the sand forms crescents, with the pointed ends pointed away from the wind; but these may "about-face" if the wind shifts. With variable winds these dunes become twisted masses.

The times of greatest wind erosion, of course, are during the tremendous sandstorms for which the deserts are so famous. A popular notion has it that people trapped in such storms are choked to death by a smothering cloud of sand churned up by the wind. Yet the truth is that, in real desert sandstorms, most of the sand is no more than a few feet off the ground. The blowing sand forms a waist-high cloud, gliding over the desert like a great moving carpet. An adult standing upright, with his head above the swirling sand, finds that he is able to breathe quite freely. Much more terrifying than sandstorms are the desert dust storms. Since dust is so much lighter than sand, the wind can raise huge clouds of it—clouds so dense that in the storm center it is as dark as night.

In a really big dust storm, the dust may be carried for almost unbelievable distances. Reddish dust whipped into the air by winds over the Sahara has been known to settle back to earth in England. In November 1933, there was a severe dust storm in the Central Plains of the United States, which includes Oklahoma and Kansas. Dust from this huge storm actually discolored the snows in New England.

Over and beyond its startling land forms and topography, the desert is a strangely fascinating place. For though it is sometimes difficult to find, a remarkable community of living things inhabits the ever-changing surface and subsurface. These plants and animals, which are adapted for survival in this fierce environment, and which do not live anywhere else in the world, are the subjects of the chapters that follow.

A Desolate Expanse of Salt

Telephone poles march to the horizon across the bleak, level Bonneville Salt Flats in Utah. Each spring runoff water from the mountains carries dissolved salts into the layers of rock beneath the flats. The saline water rises to the surface and evaporates, adding more salt to the existing billion-ton deposit.

A DESERT DOWNPOUR drenches cacti, which seem to welcome the precious water with open arms. A storm like this may well be the area's only rainfall for a whole year, yet it is over in a short time. Long awaited, the rain may evaporate as it touches the parched ground or wash away in vicious flash floods.

2
Water—the Eternal Problem

In most parts of the world, people, animals and plants can take water for granted. The heavens dependably deliver it to the earth, lakes store it, streams transport it, plants and oceans evaporate it back into the atmosphere, and all living things use it.

But the situation in the desert is very different. Water—at least rain water—is almost an accident. Now and then a storm, blown off course, clips through climatic barriers that usually divert it to temperate regions and unloads thousands of tons of rain (*opposite*). Even then, on a really hot day, the torrent can evaporate on the way down so that not a drop ever touches the thirsting earth. A parched traveler can look up at a cloud-blackened sky and see rain pouring down, but the desert's hot air prevents it from ever reaching him. A rainstorm sometimes falls on one side of a dry basin and leaves the other side untouched; such a thing as a widespread desert rain is almost unknown. So is a gentle rain. When rain does fall, it arrives in violent downpours, lasting perhaps less than an hour. But the surface of the baked ground is nearly waterproof; it sheds water in a very short time.

Storms: Few and Far Between

Deserts are generally defined as areas with an annual rainfall of 10 inches or less. The charts below compare the average desert rainfall with that in other areas; each drop represents two inches of rain. The figures are averages taken over a period of years. Desert storms are infrequent; a hamlet in the Sahara, averaging five inches a year, once went 11 years between rains. Rain can be severe; a downpour (*right*) can dump a year's average rainfall in minutes.

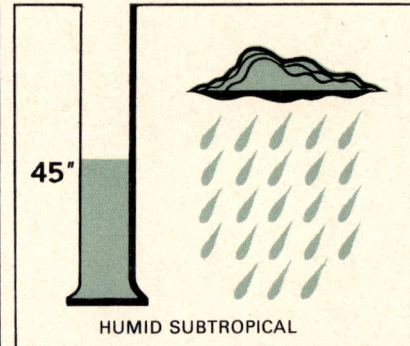
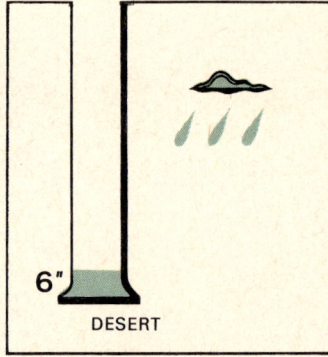

Usually a little more rain is caught by projecting mountains than by the slopes and flats of desert valleys. The water collects quickly in canyons and rushes down the dry, steep-walled stream beds. As it passes the mouth of a canyon, the water spreads out over the level ground in the shape of a fan. If it has been even a moderate rain, water may pour across the flats as a thin, solid sheet.. This flow can wash away any campsites, roads, plants or animal burrows that lie in its path. In a heavy rainstorm the water picks up sand, dust and debris and becomes laden with mud. This dense, muddy mixture can cause even more terrible destruction than water alone. There is nothing to stop such a thunderous flash flood as it tears downhill, and nothing does stop it. Once, in the Mojave Desert of the American Southwest, a flood carried a heavy locomotive more than a mile off its tracks and then buried it in the mud.

A few hours after a desert cloudburst, nothing is left but damp mud splitting and cracking in the sun. The water disappears quickly; most of it evaporates, but a little soaks into the ground and eventually seeps down into the store of underground water that can be found even under the desert. Only rarely, in river valleys such as the Nile

Rain: Too Much or Too Little

Two views of the same scene, one at the height of a flash flood and the other scant hours later, show one problem of the desert—its inability to hold the waters of a rare storm. Rain, unable to soak into the sun-hardened ground, collects in a gully (*near right*). With brutal force it spews along this channel out onto the desert flats. Hours later, the only souvenirs of the flood are a few damp spots (*far right*).

and the Colorado, does any desert water have a chance of reaching the sea, as does much of the water that falls in more temperate parts of the world.

In nondesert regions, a river is fed by tributary streams and by underground water so that it grows larger and larger as it runs toward the sea. But a river crossing the desert loses water by evaporation. Often its supply is further cut by farmers who use it for irrigation. Therefore this stream actually gets smaller as it goes along and often peters out in some interior basin. In rare cases a desert stream actually reaches the sea, but it gets there much reduced in size and heavily loaded with chemicals that have not evaporated.

Because of the chancy nature of desert rains, generations of animals may come and go without ever experiencing a rainstorm. In any particular place the entire rainfall for a whole year may come in one cloudburst. Annual statistics for rainfall on the desert are meaningless. At a dry spot near Tucson, Arizona, for instance, the average yearly rainfall is 10.7 inches a year. But over a 50-year period, the area received as little as 5.55 inches one year and as much as 24.2 another year. Such variation makes it impossible to predict how much rain will fall in a year, though such predictions are reasonably accurate in wetter parts of the world.

As chancy as they are, rains are still the biggest source of desert water and therefore what keeps most animals and plants alive. But they are not the only source. The occasional oases—naturally wet areas—are green havens that can support life far out into the encircling brown of the desert. The largest oases are on the banks of desert rivers like the Colorado, the Nile and the Indus, whose sources are in far-off, snowy mountains.

There are other green oases, however, not formed by rivers. On the Sahara, for example, there are a number of narrow ribbonlike oases that stretch for 50 miles, and one—the Street of Palms—that is about 500 miles long. These oases are formed by underground water that, because of the structure of the underlying earth, comes close enough to the surface of the land to nourish plants. Smaller ones occur wherever the ground water comes out on the surface in a spring or a seep. Usually this water appears at canyon mouths or at the edge of former mountains where bedrock rises close to the surface of the land.

Even hot springs, which are fairly common in volcanic areas, are good shelters for animals and plants. In the 19th Century, one of the main overland trails into California cut through the Nevada desert at Black Rock, where a cluster of boiling, somewhat sulphurous springs was the only watering point for many miles. The "forty-niners," toiling across the country in their covered wagons, had to barricade the springs to keep their thirsty oxen from scalding their mouths until water could be cooled enough for them to drink.

There is still another source of water on the desert, whose importance was not realized until a few years ago. This source is dew. When an Israeli scientist, Shmuel Duvdevani, began measuring dew, he found that in many areas it could add up to 10 inches of water a year. To his surprise he also learned that, except in extreme desert country, there is as much dew on arid lands as there is in humid coastal regions.

Dew is caused by moisture in the air that condenses in the early morning when the humidity is high but the temperature is still low. In humid places there is sometimes no dew because the temperature does not get down low enough at night. Thus, dry Tucson, Arizona, may get a heavier fall of dew than wet Pasadena, California.

Duvdevani's studies suggested that dew could account for the puzzling fact that crops that grow low to the ground, like tomatoes and watermelons, can prosper in dry areas where there has been practically no rainfall.

It is quite possible that research on dew may lead the way to the cultivation of large areas where there is not enough water to supply the sizable amounts needed for conventional irrigation. And it is equally possible, though nobody has thoroughly investigated the question, that many desert plants and animals have all along supplemented their meager water supply with dew.

Wherever new water comes, life is revolutionized. In the desert of Iraq, up to 1953, the nomadic tribes and their sheep shared the water from just 180 shallow wells. As the grazing seasons advanced, these few watering places became crowded, food became scarce, fighting broke out between rival sheiks. Then, the United Nations introduced modern well-digging equipment. As these new wells were brought in, pastures were extended and, for the first time in centuries, the tribesmen's precarious life became secure.

A Trick of the Desert Air

Veils of rain fall from purplish storm clouds bunched over the Sahara—but the desert below remains dry. This phenomenon, known as phantom rain, occurs when the superheated and extremely dry air that shimmers over the sand meets and evaporates the falling rain before it can reach the desert floor.

3
Plant Life on the Arid Land

A BOUQUET of lavender sand verbenas and green creosote bushes, brought to bloom by a brief rainy season, enlivens the Borrego Desert in Southern California. Gum and resin on the leaves of the verbenas seal in water and enable these plants to withstand droughts better than most desert shrubs.

The desert presents two enormous problems to anything trying to live on it—extreme dryness and intense heat. Plants that grow in temperate climates could never survive under these harsh conditions. Still there is a great variety of species that have developed the ability to thrive there.

Since all plants need water to live and grow, desert plant life must be able to escape during prolonged periods of drought into a state of "sleep," or rest, which requires very little water. During such times the desert is drab and dead. Trees and shrubs are leafless and gaunt, and even cacti are shriveled.

But the miracle of rain transforms the scene almost overnight into a fertile garden (*opposite*). Leaves pop out of naked twigs; flower buds swell among thorns and spines. The bare ground is quickly carpeted with green shoots and blades, pushing through the soaked soil from long-hidden bulbs and seeds. For a few glorious weeks the desert is in bloom. But soon the leaves begin to wither, the fruits and seeds fall, the flowers disappear and until the next rain the sleeplike state returns for many desert plants.

Another notable thing about desert vegetation is its variety in form and type. In climates more favorable for plant growth, there is keen competition for space; some plants survive and eliminate others by shading them out. In the desert the primary struggle of the plants is for water rather than for space and light as in the forest. There is very little of the "layering" of plant types that is typical in the tropical rain forest. When a forest is destroyed by cutting or by burning, new light-loving species—annuals, bushes and low trees—spring up, and it may take decades for the forest to regain its original appearance. If a desert-plant community is wiped out, the first plants that spring up are almost always the very same species that have been destroyed.

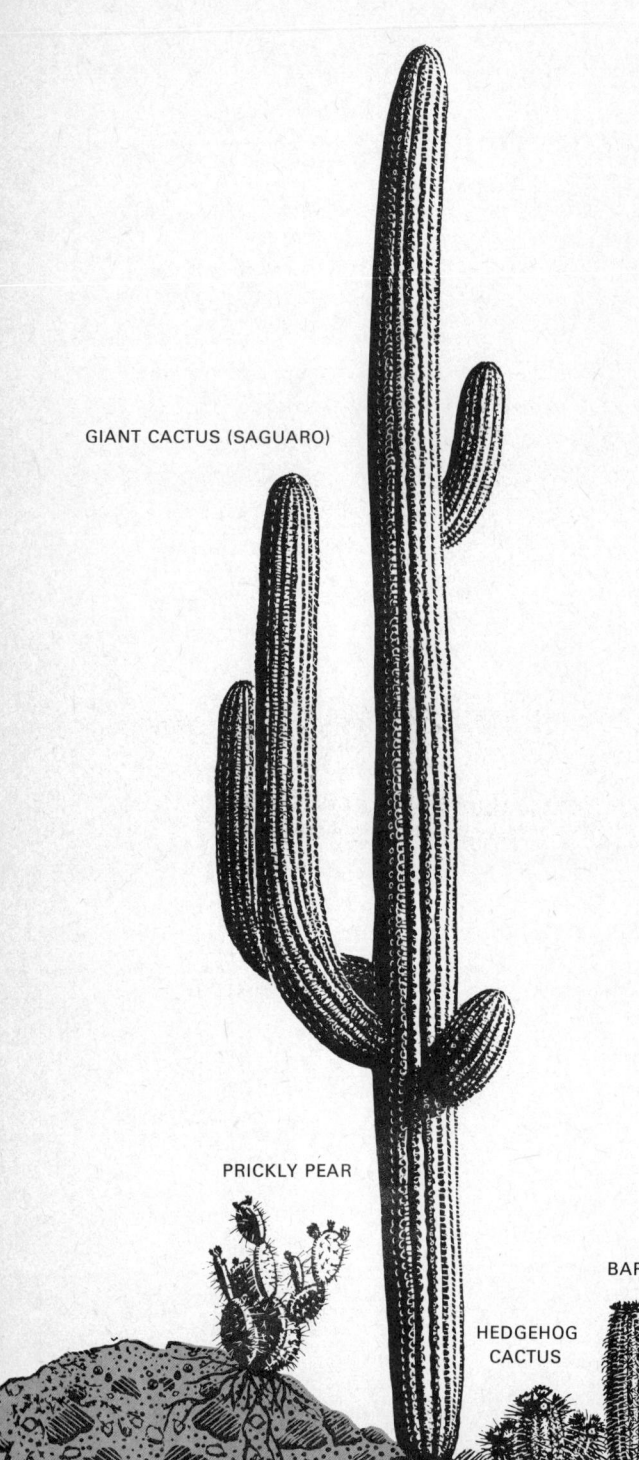

But all types of desert plants must deal with the problem of drought. They do it in two ways. One group, the so-called "drought evaders," dies off in each dry season, leaving behind hardy seeds that will sprout when the next rain falls. A different group, the "drought resisters," manages to stay alive during the dry period by growing at a very slow rate. The giant saguaro cactus, for instance, may grow only three feet in 50 years, but can live to the ripe old age of 200.

The drought resisters have evolved a variety of techniques that help them to avoid drying out. Some of them, the succulents, store up large quantities of water during the infrequent rains. On the American desert the best-known succulents are the cacti, which come in a wide range of sizes from 50-foot-high saguaros to tiny round plants the size of a thumbnail.

Nearly everything about a cactus is designed to help it store water. Most of them are shaped like a ball or a column, which prevents water loss by exposing the smallest possible surface area to the dry air. Since leaves lose a great deal of water by evaporation, cacti are usually leafless except when they are young. Even then the leaves are tiny. To prevent nibbling by animals tempted by the plants' juicy flesh, many cacti are covered with sharp, menacing spines.

Some cacti are pleated like an accordion so that they can quickly expand and soak up water when it rains. During dry spells they live on their stored water, gradually shrinking and becoming wrinkled again.

All of these plants collect water through their roots, which are specially adapted for absorbing great quantities of moisture in a short period. As we have seen, even when it rains very little water soaks into the sun-baked desert floor. To get an adequate sup-

The Roots of Survival

To take full advantage of scanty rainfall, desert plants have evolved several distinct types of root systems. Trees such as the mesquite tap underground water with deep-reaching roots many times as long as the above-ground growth. The roots of other plants, such as the cereus, store water in underground bulbs. Still others, such as the cacti, have a web of wide-ranging roots fanning out close to the surface, where 97 per cent of the infrequent rain remains.

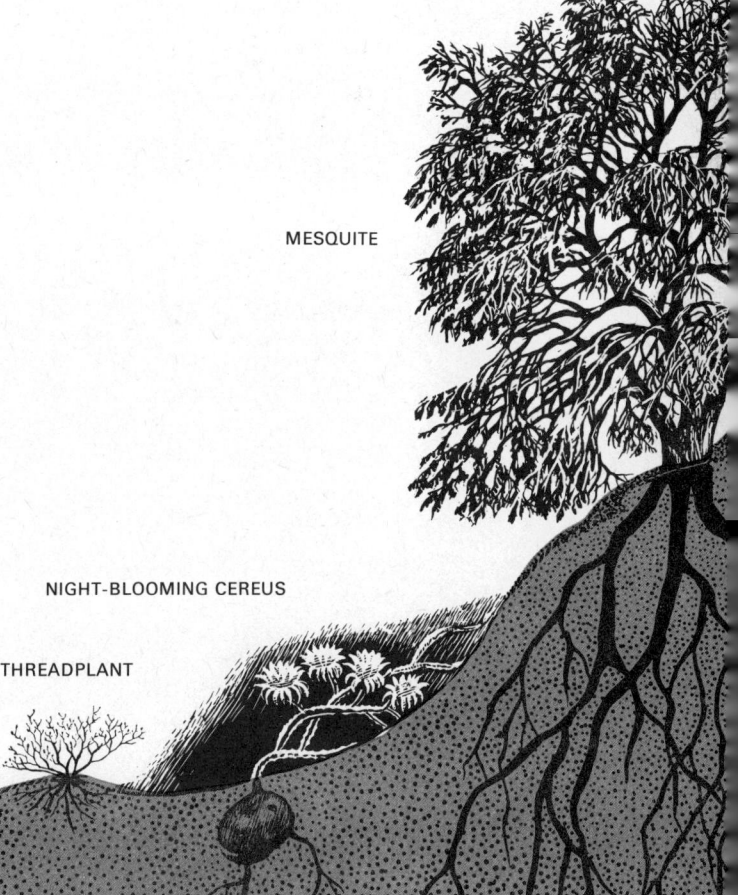

MESQUITE

OCOTILLO PRIMROSE NIGHT-BLOOMING CEREUS

THREADPLANT

A Widely Spaced Grove

A cluster of acacia trees grows in a semiarid African savanna. If these trees were any closer, they could not survive, for their far-ranging roots need the space to gather the sparse rainfall of an area where nine-month droughts are not infrequent.

ply of water, the cacti spread their roots in a wide area just under the surface. Saguaro roots, for instance, may reach out as far as 50 feet on either side of the plant's stem to drain water from a large area.

In years past, the saguaro was used in many valuable ways by desert Indians like the Papagos and Pimas. They mashed it up for liquids in time of drought. They ate its fruit, which has a red pulp resembling that of a watermelon when fresh; the saguaro pulp can also be preserved in a syrupy form for many months. Its juice made an alcoholic drink when fermented, its seeds a kind of butter. The giant stems made lodgepoles for Indian dwellings, and even in death its dried remains were a source of fuel.

Among the 1,000-odd other and smaller cacti are many with odd shapes and reputations. The stout, unbranched barrel cactus is supposed to have supplied a water source for parched travelers, but it wasn't quite that easy. To get liquid, the top of the plant must first be chopped off; then the pulpy interior must be mashed until a liquid (unpleasant-tasting at that) is obtained. This is hard, perspiring work, and besides, the bar-

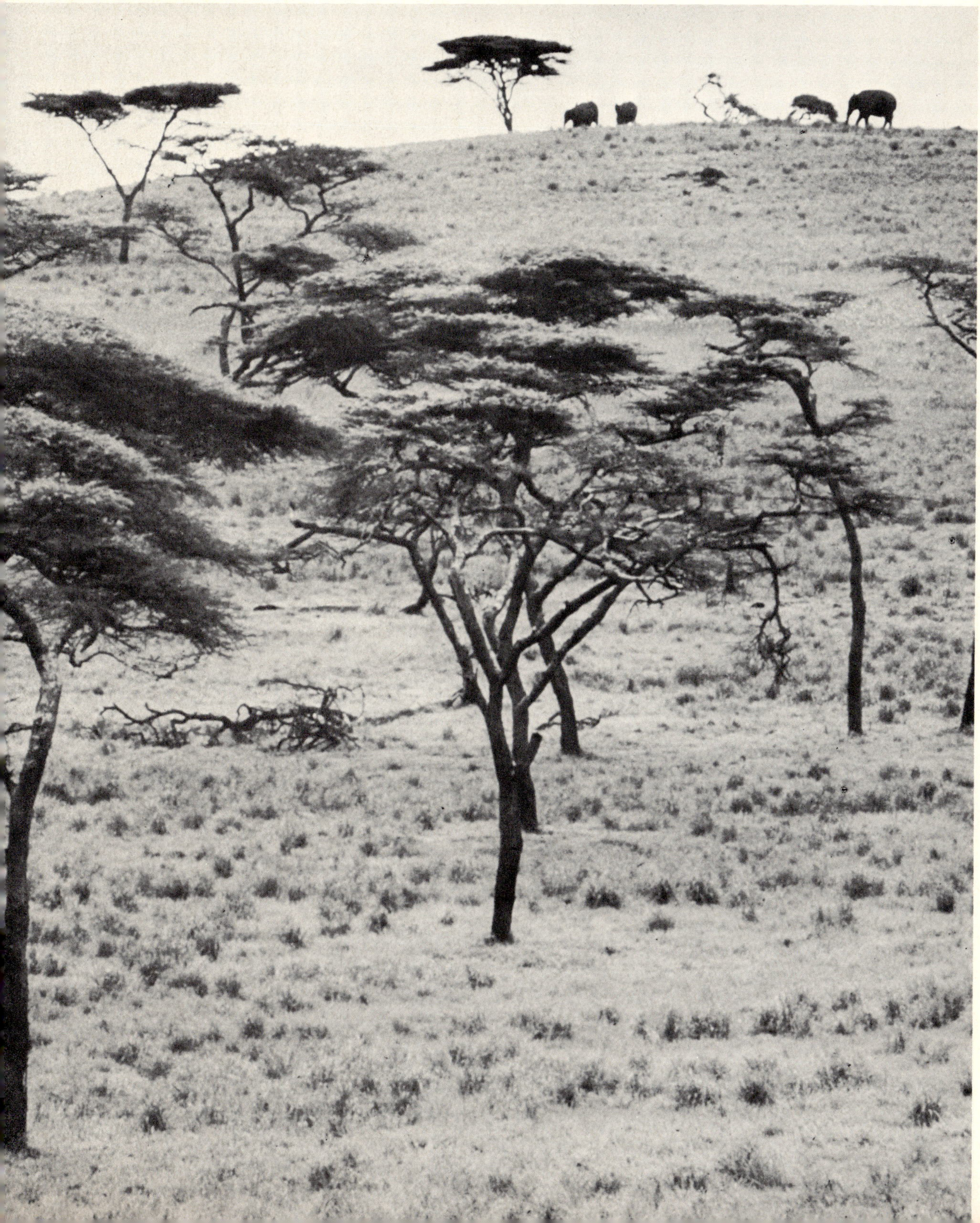

rel cactus bristles with spines so tough and sharp that the Indians used to use them for fishhooks.

The squat, branched hedgehog cactus, on the other hand, produces from its brilliant blooms a delicious, easily picked, strawberry-red fruit. The many-branched organ cactus is named for its resemblance to a pipe organ, and the flame-tipped staghorn cholla, close relative of the prickly pear, sometimes bears branches like the antlers of a deer. The teddybear cactus, or jumping cholla, has easily detached joints that seem to leap at passersby. But the cactus merely sticks to whatever brushes against its barbs, and it cannot really "jump" at all.

The trees of the desert have developed ways of surviving drought quite different from those of the cacti. Instead of storing water, they send enormously long taproots deep into the soil to reach a source of underground water. A common American desert tree, the mesquite, sometimes sends down a root 100 feet long. But how do the young mesquites survive without water while they are growing such long roots? The mesquite solves this problem in an interesting way: the young tree grows hardly at all on the surface. During its early months, it is practically all root; it will not grow above ground until its root locates a good water source.

The mesquite is a great steadying influence on sand dunes. Instead of being smothered by the drifts that pile up around it, it sends out many shoots that emerge above the dune. These branches break the wind, causing more sand to accumulate, and the plant branches farther. In time, around each mesquite there is a hard sand mound, held firm and immovable by the tree underneath. The branches that show may be mere switches supporting the leaves, but great limbs are buried in the sand. In northern Mexico and from southern Texas to Arizona, woodcutters yank out these buried limbs, and a single dune may yield half a truckload of mesquite, one of the world's finest firewoods.

The mesquite is in the family of the pea and the bean, with its flinty seeds enclosed in a pod. If the seeds are simply planted in the soil, few of them will grow, even if well watered. But if the pods are eaten by cattle, deer or other browsers, whole seeds that pass through the digestive tract sprout readily. The animal's digestive juices seem to remove the glassy seed coat, allowing water to penetrate and start germination. The process serves nature as a good method of seed dispersal, for manure helps get seedlings started. Across the world, in the Kalahari Desert in southwestern Africa, a similar process takes place: the tough seeds of the huge baobab tree sprout more readily after passing through the digestive tract of the baboon.

Seeds of some other trees of the American desert washes, among them the ironwood, smoke tree, and blue paloverde, also require bruising before they can germinate. In Death Valley the seedlings of the smoke tree do not sprout around the parent tree but rather 150

STEM DURING DROUGHT

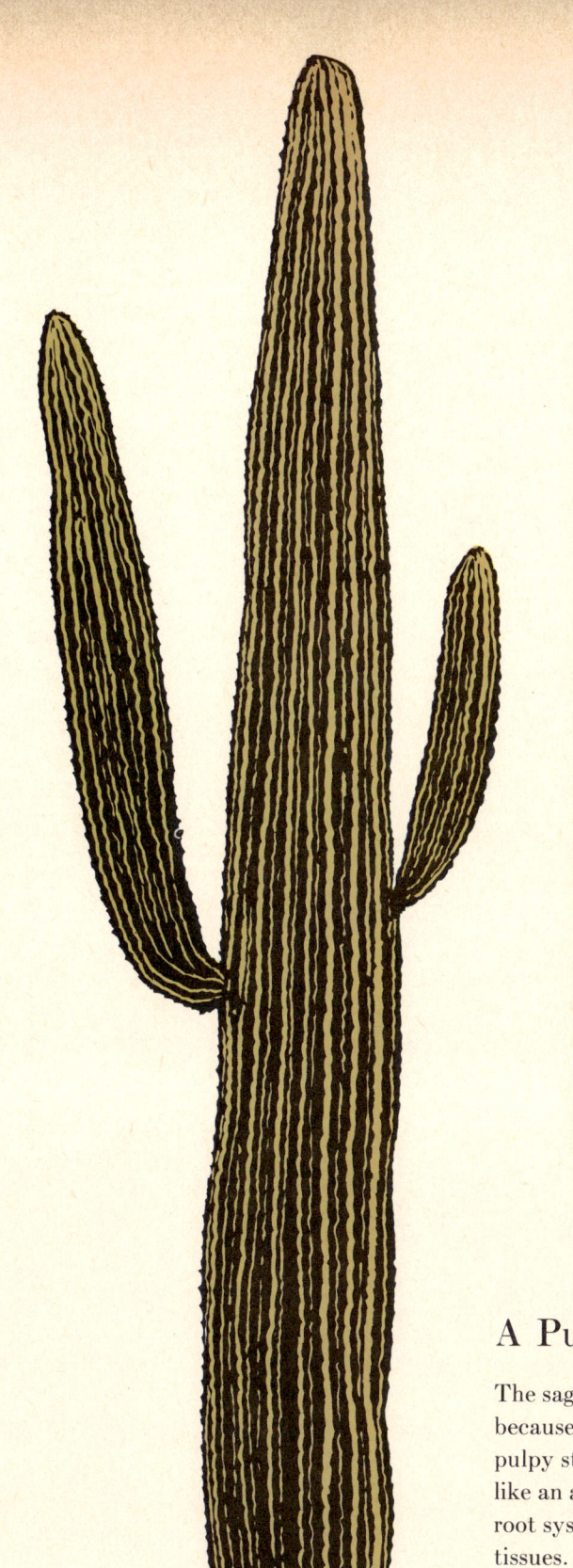

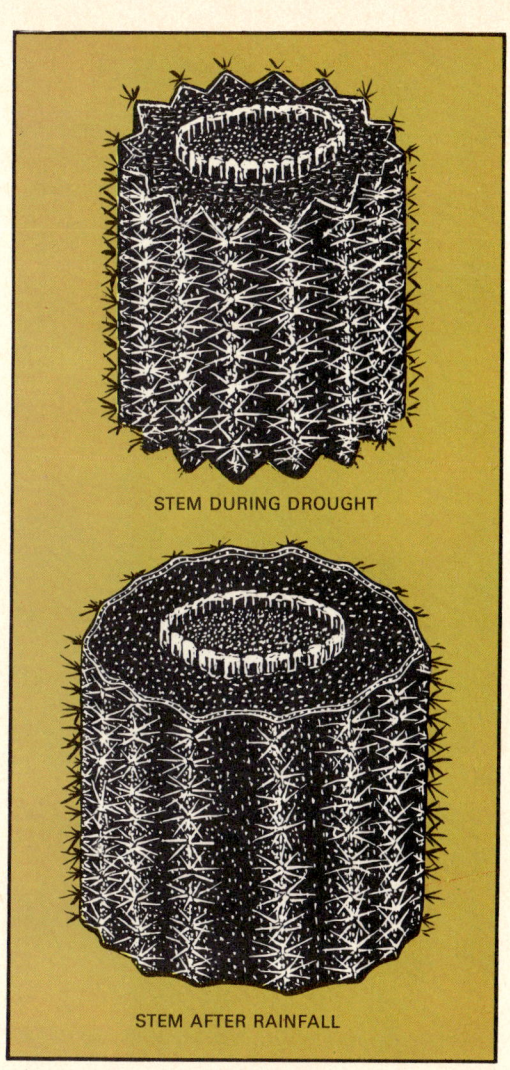

STEM AFTER RAINFALL

A Pulpy Reservoir of Water

The saguaro, or giant cactus, survives in the desert because it can store vast amounts of water in its pulpy stem. During a dry season, the stem folds up like an accordion *(top)*. When it rains, a wide-ranging root system brings in water, swelling the storage tissues. Well adapted to withstand droughts, mature saguaros have been known to live more than 200 years, reach heights of 50 feet and weights of 10 tons.

to 300 feet away, downgrade. Seeds carried that far are chipped to admit water through their hard coats; if they travel much farther they are crushed.

These odd conditions for germination are no more curious than the conditions certain other trees must have before they will grow properly. For example, the Joshua tree of the Mojave is a spooky-looking yucca that lives for hundreds of years and may reach a height of 25 feet. It lives only at desert elevations above 2,500 feet, where the summers are scorching and the winters cold.

When planted in lower desert lands or along the California coast, the small seedlings thrive for two or three years and then stop growing. But experiments with some of these young Joshua trees have proved that they can be made to grow vigorously again if they are put in a cold chamber with the temperature near freezing for a couple of months. If it is to remain healthy, the Joshua tree needs periods of low temperature when it becomes dormant for a time.

Like cacti, many desert trees do not bear water-wasting leaves. The paloverde tree, for instance, has leaves only one twenty-fifth of an inch across, and even these are shed during a drought. Most trees could not survive without leaves because the leaves make chlorophyll, the green pigment that plants use to manufacture their food. The paloverde tree, however, has a supply of chlorophyll in its stem, so that it can continue to make food even after it has lost its leaves.

Leaf shedding is carried even further by the long-branched ocotillo plant. When its branches are in full leaf, it needs a great deal of water, but it sheds its leaves at the first hint of a drought. A tough armor of resin-filled cells in the bark then protects the plant against water loss. In an unusually wet season the plant may keep its leaves for months or it may grow several sets of leaves in response to scattered rains. Ocotillos are so sensitive to small differences in the soil's water content that one plant may have all its leaves and another, within a few yards of it, in a slightly drier spot, may be bare.

Other plants survive by drying up between rains. They keep alive because they have specially adapted roots, tubers or bulbs that serve as underground containers of food and water. The size of some of these buried plant treasures is astonishing. The night-blooming

Fragile Beauty in the Desert

Despite harsh conditions, delicate and brightly colored flowers can bloom in the desert. The flowers of the giant cactus (*far left*) escape the heat by opening only at night. Bronzed chenopods (*middle*) grow in scattered clumps; they consume all available water, and nothing can grow between them. The hedgehog cactus (*top right*) bears strawberry-flavored fruit, while the barrel cactus (*bottom right*), despite its gentle beauty, has curved spines so tough that American Indians used them for fishhooks.

Bristling Protection

Thorns—presumably a defense of desert plants against animals—resemble each other, but they have evolved differently. Ocotillo barbs are the stem and midrib of modified leaves, but the spines of the prickly pear and saguaro cacti grow directly from the plants' outer skins, as do the spurs of the puncture vine. The spikes of the crucifix thorn are leafless branches, while the prickles of the thistle are sharp leaf edges.

OCOTILLO

PUNCTURE VINE

PRICKLY PEAR

CRUCIFIX THORN

SAGUARO

WAVY THISTLE

cereus has a water-storage container underground in the form of a huge bulb, which can weigh 40 pounds when it is filled with water.

On one African desert there grows a spindly vine that the Bushmen call *bi*. This vine springs out of a great underground tuber, which may grow as big as a basketball. Bushmen carefully note the location of *bi* plants during the wet season. Later, when the plants disappear during the dry season, the natives can go back to the places where they saw vines and dig up the tubers for water.

Since a sufficient supply of water is a matter of life and death to a plant, the struggle for water is often deadly. Once established, some plants keep others from growing up and competing for water through their spreading roots, which drain the soil and prevent nearby growth.

Some desert plants actually use a kind of chemical warfare to preserve themselves. It has long been known, for instance, that even in a wet season no other plants grow underneath a brittlebush. Scientists wondered how the shrub kept its neighbors away, and decided to study the question. They took some leaves from a brittlebush and found that they poisoned any seedlings growing near them. Eventually the scientists discovered the exact chemical composition of the poison, and they were able to make the poison in the laboratory. They found that only the brittlebush and the sunflower resisted the poison.

More than half of all the species of perennial succulents, trees and shrubs share the tendency to produce thorns. While thorniness is by no means found only in desert plants, it is common enough to be listed as a quality important for survival in arid conditions. Just why so many plants are thorny is not known, but it is significant that very few species in Australia possess thorns. Every other desert has—or once had—native hoofed animals that browse the twigs and stems of perennials during droughts. Australia has only kangaroos and they are not aggressive browsers. The thorns are probably a primary defense of the plants against browsing animals: desert plants cannot afford to lose foliage—which in moist climates is more easily regrown. There are some species, always thorny in the desert, that produce no thorns at all when reared in the secure, humid protection of a greenhouse. But the mechanism by which dryness stimulates thorn production, while dampness halts it, has not yet been figured out.

The drought evaders make up the largest group of desert plants. They are annuals that solve the problem of drought by simply avoiding it and survive from rainfall to rainfall, not as plants but as seeds. Since the annuals do not really have to deal with the problem of drought the way other desert plants do, they look quite similar to the annuals one sees in temperate parts of the world. Their leaves are not hairy or waxy, and they have no water-storage containers or deep taproots. They live on the water supply of the moment, sending up large and gaudy flowers and providing for the future with a crop of seeds.

The seed crop is always far greater than the minimum that would be required to carry a species through a drought. But it is not really wasted, for the billions of seeds that fall into the desert soil are the basic, staple support of many of the animals that live there.

The annuals prosper in sand, for moisture goes deeper there. The seeds are easily washed or blown to their proper depth in this loose soil, but on hard surfaces they have a difficult time finding a footing, and most are washed or blown away. For this reason, relatively few annuals grow on hard desert soil. A comfortable location for them is under a perennial bush or tree, where they are sheltered and protected in its moisture-conserving shade.

While the growing annual plants themselves are scarcely different from their relatives in well-watered climates, their seeds show some specialized attributes. The all-important issue, from the standpoint of the seeds, is when to germinate. In the course of evolution, desert plants have developed the ability to respond to the exact set of conditions most likely to lead to their successful growth. This was demonstrated many years ago by Forrest Shreve of the Carnegie Desert Laboratory at Tucson, Arizona. He observed that some of the desert plants there germinated after winter rains coming in from the Northwest Pacific, others only after summer rains from the southwestern monsoon coming up from the Gulf of Mexico, and that still others had two germinating periods—one after each rainy season.

In an effort to find out what makes seeds

Plants' Roles in a Dry Land

The clumps of vegetation dotting this sun-singed desert soften the bleakness of the landscape with color. But the plants also guard against further erosion by acting as windbreaks, and their root systems anchor the sparse soil. Desert animals use the plants for life-preserving food and shade.

germinate at exactly the right time, Frits Went, an American botanist, made painstaking studies of seeds from the Joshua Tree National Monument east of Los Angeles. In this desert there are two periods of rainfall each year, and a different group of plants germinates and blooms in each wet season. The botanist skimmed some soil that contained both kinds of seeds off the desert and took it to his greenhouse. There he observed the effects of different amounts of water and different temperatures on various samples.

The first thing Went discovered was that none of the seeds would germinate unless he applied at least a half inch of water or, better still, an inch. Since the soil was just as wet after a tenth of an inch as it was after an inch, he concluded that the seeds must have a chemical coating that kept them from sprouting until it was washed away by a good deal of water. On the desert this coating would keep the seeds from sprouting after a small shower, which could never support the plants until maturity. He also found that temperature determined when certain seeds would sprout. None of the seeds that normally sprouted at winter temperatures would sprout at summer temperatures, and none of the summer flowers would sprout at winter temperatures.

Even under the proper conditions, some of the seeds failed to germinate. On the desert these resistant seeds probably serve as insurance if for some reason the early sprouts fail. Thus at no time is the soil's seed bank emptied completely. Some of these seeds may survive for as long as half a dozen years, thus insuring that there will still be some seeds of each species left to sprout when enough rain finally does fall.

Of course, plants are not the only life in the desert. The plants are fertilized by numbers of insects. And the insects in turn are eaten by a number of desert animals. In fact, the desert plants are the base of a whole pyramid of life. Because so many kinds of plants have adapted so successfully to the harsh and arid desert environment, life is possible for the desert's large and varied community of animals.

Sweets from a Thorny Plant

Brightly blossomed and barrel-shaped, the candy cactus is one of the desert's edible plants. In addition to being a source of water, many cacti bear fleshy fruits that are eaten by various desert animals. Humans mix the meaty center of the candy cactus with sugar to make a treat called "cactus candy."

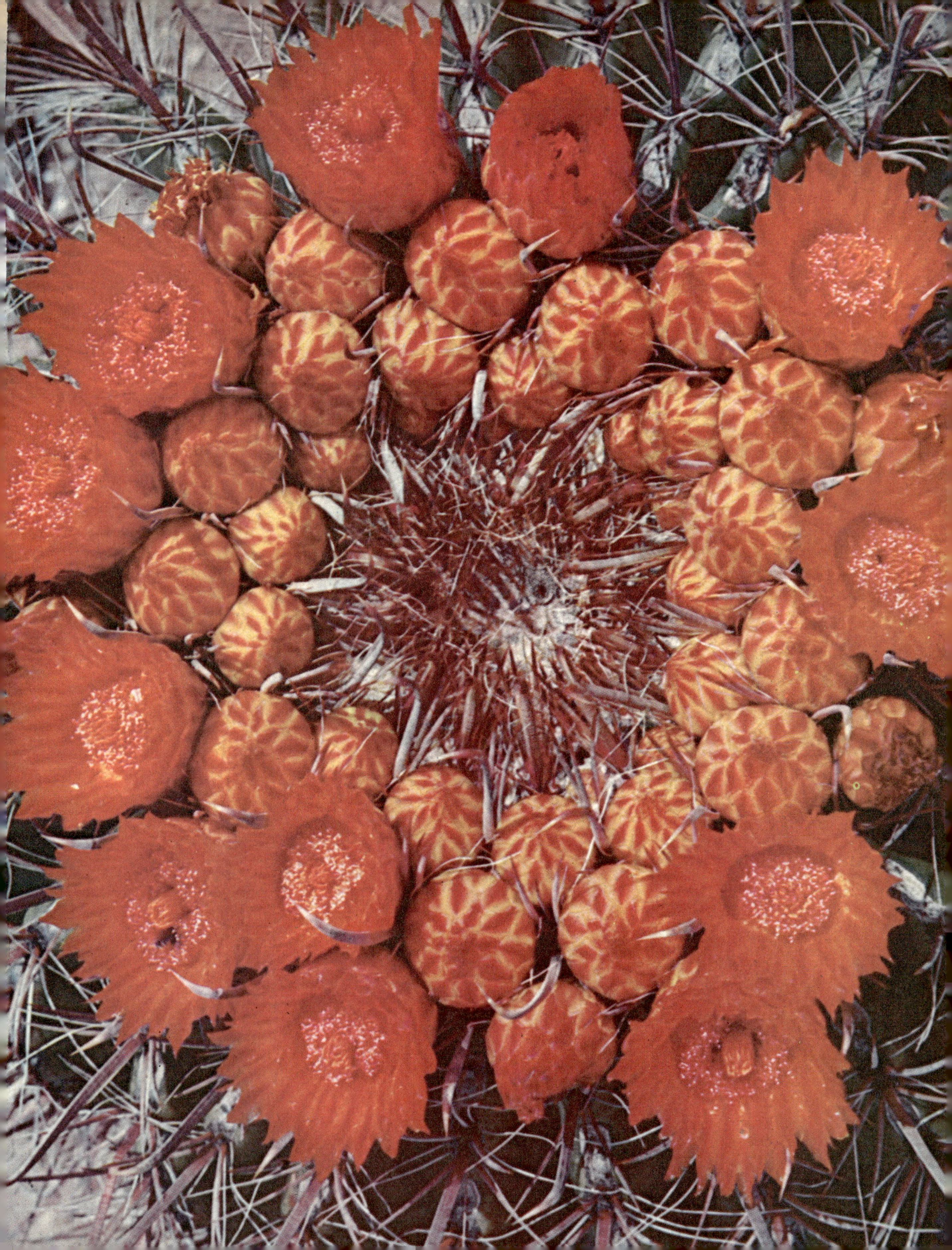

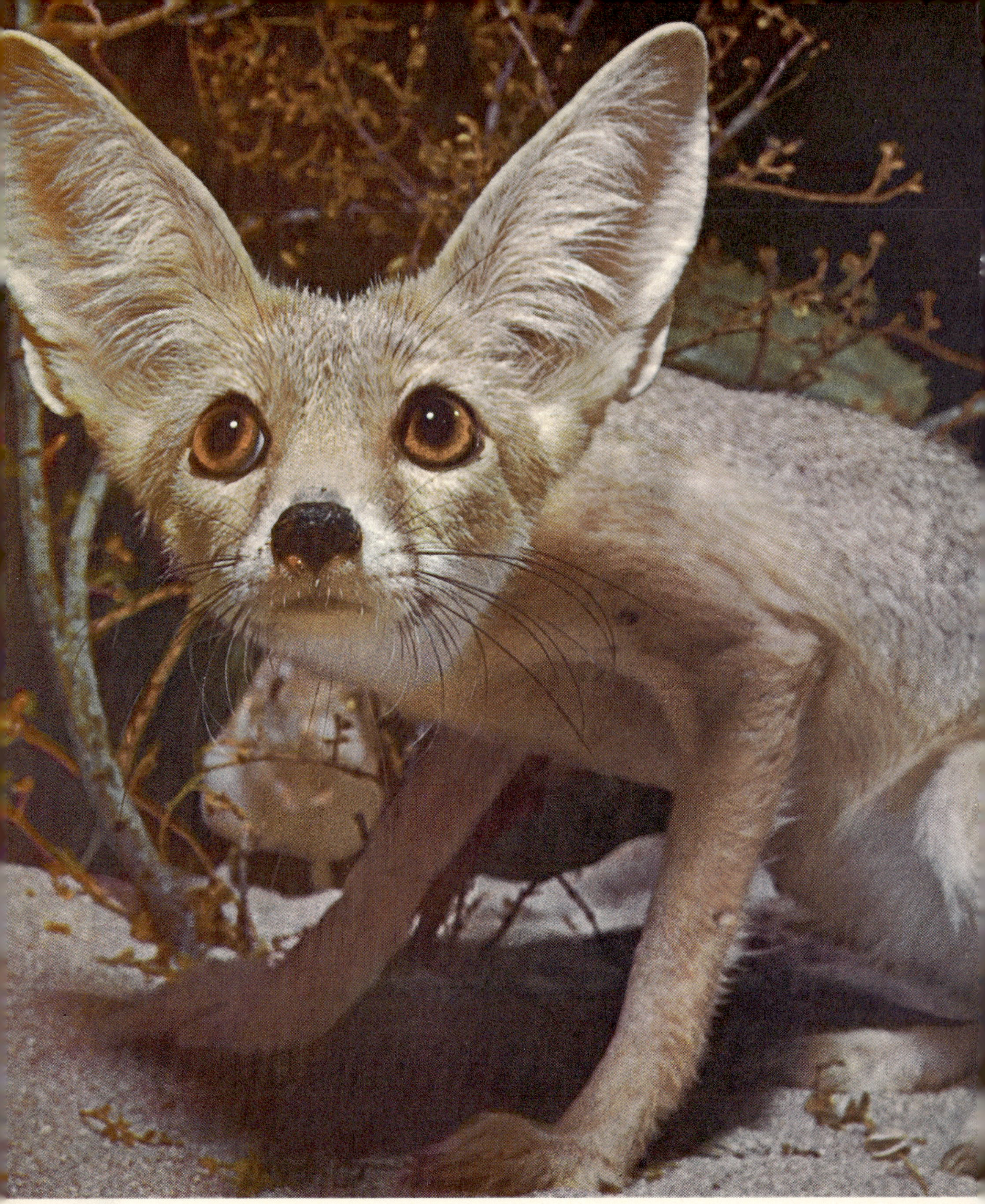

4
The World of Desert Animals

The deathly stillness of a summer desert at noon is an illusion, for the dry land teems with life. Though they are often almost invisible, a host of living things—insects, spiders, fishes, snakes, rabbits, cats, rats, birds and foxes—bustle about their business despite the cruel climate. In fact, relatives of all of the more familiar temperate-zone animals are present on the desert, along with many unfamiliar species.

As with all other animals, the food that keeps desert animals alive must start as plant life. This is because only green plants can manufacture food from inorganic, or lifeless, materials. Using the energy of the sun, plants combine carbon dioxide from the air with water from the soil to make sugars and starch. This plant material is the basic food of all animals; some eat the plants and others eat the plant eaters.

From this it follows that the plants growing in any area determine the kind and number of animals that can live there. There can be no meat eaters, for instance, if there are no seeds to feed the small rodents that the predatory animals eat.

On the desert there are two phases of

STIFFLY ALERT, a kit fox listens for telltale sounds that help it locate a victim. The kit fox is well equipped for hunting in the cool of the desert night; its large, sensitive ears catch the rustling sound made by moving rodents. Once a prey is located, the kit fox uses its speed to catch its meal.

plant growth—one in the period of rainfall when leaves, flowers, seeds and fruits are in good supply, and the other in the long periods of drought when the only plant foods available are the stems, roots, and drought-resistant leaves. The dangerous time for animals is the drought period, and the animals that live in the desert are those that have found a way to adjust to, or avoid, the long dry spells.

Following the first good rains, plants start growing and the desert crawls and buzzes with an enormous number and variety of insects—beetles, ants, wasps, moths and butterflies. They feed heavily on the flourishing plants, reproduce and then most of them die. But the insects leave behind a rich supply of eggs, and also of pupae, the unformed insect adolescent. The eggs and pupae serve as the main food for many birds, reptiles and even some mammals.

But insects are not the only animals that live this on-and-off kind of life. Hard as it is to believe, there are actually aquatic creatures that flourish on the desert for a short time after a heavy rain. Once after Bicycle

Dry Lake in the Mojave Desert had been without rain for 25 years, a cloudburst filled it up. The shallow water was soon packed with tiny shrimp *(page 67)*. Apparently the shrimp had lain dormant as eggs in the parched, salty soil for a quarter of a century and then hatched in the 110° F. water of the temporary lake. Before the lake dried up they had laid eggs to await the next rain.

Fish, unlike shrimp, require a continuing supply of water; rare as this is in the desert, there is still enough to support about 20 species of desert fish in the Western United

Mammals Suited to Dry Land

Two mammals that have adapted well to the rigors of desert life—the camel *(above)* and the ass *(below)* —trek across arid wastelands. Both animals are prized by man as beasts of burden because of their ability to survive for long periods with little food or water, for their capacity to withstand the desert's heat, and for the ease with which they can be tamed.

A Rodent's Terror

Wholly engrossed in its food, a hungry badger munches on a desert iguana. While it prefers rodents, the badger will eat other animals when its favorite food is scarce. The badger is an excellent digger and can burrow deeply to catch its prey in their underground lairs.

States and northern Mexico. Some of these species can only barely survive. The Devil's Hole pupfish, a minnow less than an inch long, dwells in only one hole of tepid water in a cave at Ash Meadows, Nevada. To save its home and prevent the species from dying off, the area was added to an adjoining National Monument in 1952. The population of the pupfish is holding steady at about 200. While the pupfish survive, seven other desert species have already become extinct; in some cases their water holes dried up, in others, competing fish were introduced.

Amphibians are far more persistent and successful desert inhabitants than fish. Because amphibians, too, die if they dry out, catch basins where water collects have their quotas of frogs, toads and even salamanders. The spadefoot toad has some of the best defenses against drought. When drought sets in, this toad keeps wet by using a horny bump on each hind foot to dig itself into damp ground. It lines this underground cell with a jellylike substance that helps to prevent water loss by evaporation. Then the toad begins a period of estivation—a sleeplike state of suspended animation that is similar to hibernation.

The toad's long sleep normally lasts about eight or nine months. A cloudburst may then soak the soil, whereupon the male toad wakes up, digs out and heads for the nearest puddle. There he calls loudly until a female wakes up and joins him. Quickly, eggs are laid and fertilized, for time is of the greatest

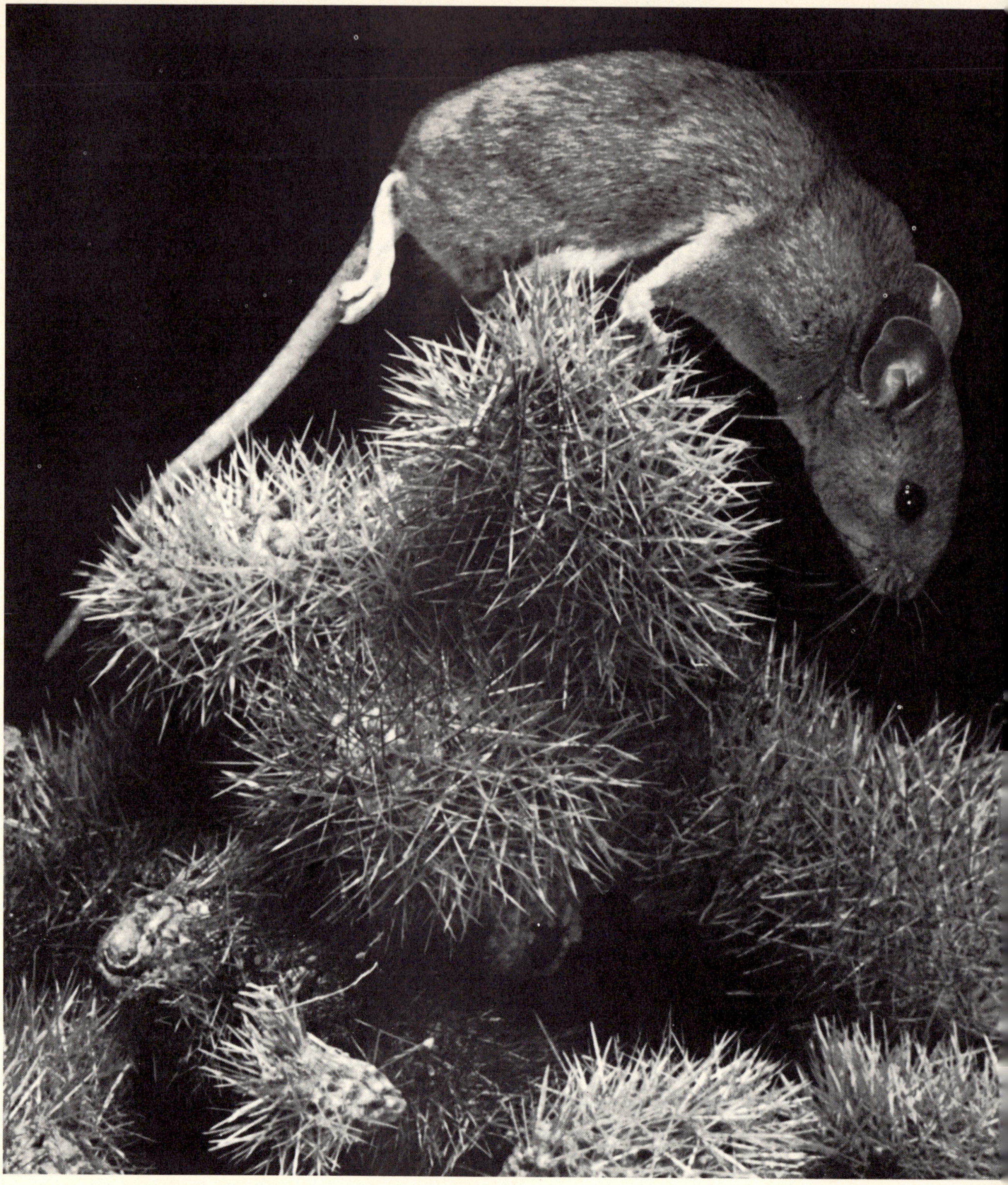

A Tasty Meal—If Caught

The pack rat protects its burrow with cactus prickles. The two-inch-high dwarf kangaroo rat uses agility to escape. With strong hind legs and a rudderlike tail, it can hop along at 17 feet per second and change direction in mid-air. Although they are hunted by many carnivores, the pack rat *(opposite)* and dwarf kangaroo rat *(above)* survive because each breeds in numbers so huge that some individuals always escape, and each has an effective defense.

importance. Tadpoles hatch out in a day or so and in a week can find their way to the mud at the bottom of their drying puddle. Within a month they are completely grown up and ready to burrow into the ground themselves, to await another rain.

Unlike many kinds of desert animals, the reptiles have a number of natural advantages for desert living, among them scaly or plated skins that resist drying. Reptiles lay their eggs in the soil, where there is usually enough dampness for them to hatch. The young are born looking like miniature adults; they do not have to go through a dangerous tadpole phase when they must live in water. The desert tortoise, which grows to be about a foot long, lives in some of the harshest parts of the Mojave Desert of southern California and the Sonoran Desert, which stretches from California through Arizona to Mexico. Helping the tortoise is its ability to convert some of its food into water, which it stores in two sacs under its shell. A pint can last a tortoise for a whole dry season.

To someone walking in the desert in daytime, lizards are probably the most conspicuous of all living things. Fast runners, like the zebra-tailed lizard, dash around the flats on their hind legs, with their front legs dangling against their chests. Spiny lizards scut-

Speedster of the Desert

The roadrunner, a desert bird of the American Southwest, rarely flies but is nimble on the ground. With large, X-shaped claws and strong legs, it can speed at up to 15 miles an hour *(opposite, top)*. By flicking its foot-long tail to one side, it can turn in mid-stride *(opposite, middle and bottom)*. The tail, when spread and raised above the bird's back *(below)*, brakes the roadrunner to a quick stop.

tle over the rocks and around the trunks of trees, hunting for insects. On stretches of sand flat, prickly horned lizards wait motionless for passing beetles and ants.

While lizards are frequently seen out in the sun during the day, they are not able to stand too much heat. Most of them collapse if their body temperatures go over 104° F., and they function best at 96° to 100°. Since they lack the built-in cooling systems supplied in mammals by sweat glands, lizards take on the temperature of their surroundings, which can reach 190° in the sun. Therefore, they keep their body temperature within tolerable limits by moving back and forth from sun to shade. These animals are very successful in determining how long it is safe for them to stay in the sun; scientists who have studied lizards have discovered that their temperatures do not change more than a few degrees.

The only poisonous lizard in the United States is the 20-inch long Gila (pronounced *hee-lah*) monster. Usually it feeds on birds' eggs and nestlings as well as small lizards and rodents. When it catches an animal, the Gila injects poison into its prey through its teeth. If animal food is not to be found, the Gila will resort to eating insects as most other lizards do.

Though there is no record of a human ever being killed by a Gila monster's bite, the experience can be painful. Despite the revulsion that many people feel for this lizard, however, it is sluggish and rarely bites people. The State of Arizona recently passed a law giving it full protection because of its interest to scientists and tourists.

Compared to the numbers of lizards, there are not a great many snakes on the desert, but those that do live there have developed admirable adaptations to help them survive. Snakes that inhabit sand dunes have nostrils equipped with valves that keep sand out when they are crawling through a dune, and their mouths are countersunk into their heads, also to prevent sand from entering.

Cold-blooded Answer to Heat

Desert reptiles such as the banded gecko lizard (*opposite*) and the racer snake (*below*) have learned to cope with the heat of the desert. Although reptiles are "cold-blooded," that is, they assume the temperature of their surroundings, they cannot survive a temperature of more than 120°. So lizards and snakes constantly seek shade during the day and confine their search for food to the cooler nights.

Though most snakes, including the poisonous species, are generally shy and retiring, some, like the little sidewinder rattlesnake, are easily aroused by fear into frantic striking activity. Both the sidewinder and the sand viper of Africa have evolved a unique way of crawling across loose sand. Touching the ground at only two points, the snake thrusts the rest of its body sideways. Its sideways motion leaves characteristic rows of parallel tracks in the sand.

The sidewinder rattlesnake roams widely and strikes at its enemies from sand-pit ambushes. In the heat of the day it twists into a coil the size of a small coffee ring, in the shadow of a bush or in the depression made by an animal hoof, but it is always on the alert for possible danger.

Another exception is the American king snake, among the most aggressive and determined of serpents whether encountered on the desert—where there are not a great many—or elsewhere. It attacks and feeds upon other snakes, including even the rattlers. When a king snake and a rattlesnake meet, the rattler usually retreats, maintaining a purely defensive attitude. If the king snake attacks, it will try to seize the rattler's neck, so the latter keeps its head low and arches the middle of its body, with which it can deliver a heavy blow by a violent sideways twist. It makes little effort to strike or bite the king snake with its fangs, for the latter is immune to rattlesnake venom.

A snake's sense of smell is aided by its forked tongue, which sends samples of air to a pair of chambers in the mouth. These chambers are lined with sensory cells that have nerve connections with the olfactory lobes of the brain, which respond to odors. When a snake flicks its forked tongue, it is testing for odors; the nostrils are not believed to contribute much to the sense of smell. Much snake behavior consists of automatic reactions to odors. Thus when a rattlesnake is exposed to the odor of a king snake, it reacts with the defensive head-down maneuver. But if the rattler's tongue is removed, this reaction does not occur, even if an aggressive king snake is brought into plain sight.

Unlike most reptiles and amphibians, desert birds show few special adaptations to their dry, hot environment. Many species completely avoid the problem by migrating. They use the desert as a breeding ground when it is moist and hospitable but leave when it gets too dry or cold. The highest temperature birds can tolerate is about 115°, and they must cool off by panting. Since panting causes a loss of water by evaporation, overheated birds must replenish their moisture. The birds that eat insects or dead animals get water in their food. But the seedeaters must have real drinking water. During dry seasons birds cluster around any open spring, and many will fly miles every day to get a drink.

The strain of raising young makes the water problem even more severe. For this reason birds rely on a very accurate timing mechanism that signals them to mate and rear their young at the time when water is most abundant. This mechanism is usually related to the length of nights. In deserts where the "wet season" comes in the spring, birds are stimulated to mate by the increasing hours of daylight. Where rainy seasons come in the fall, the birds start to mate as the hours of daylight shorten.

But such well-timed patterns of behavior are no help in deserts where rain is not predictable. There birds must be prepared to mate and raise families as soon as the rare rains start. In central Australia many small insect-eating birds remain paired for years, and the moment the rain starts falling they rush to build a nest. The female produces eggs and starts incubating them. No one knows quite what triggers the birds' nesting behavior, but it seems to be partly the actual sight and feel of raindrops.

Desert birds eat a variety of things, from seeds and insects to snakes. The roadrunner, a clownish-looking bird that runs on the ground more than it flies, is a great snake catcher (*pages 58 and 59*). Once it kills its prey, the bird starts to swallow it. Often the snake is too long for the bird to get down

Useful Arthropods

Desert arthropods such as the scorpion, the whip scorpion and the sun spider are important in arid lands. Since they feed exclusively on insects—often consuming an amount equal to their own weight daily—they help keep down the insect population. Arthropods themselves are vital to the diet of many desert animals. In addition to being food, arthropods such as the spider, which is over 80 per cent liquid, give birds like the elf owl all the water they ever need.

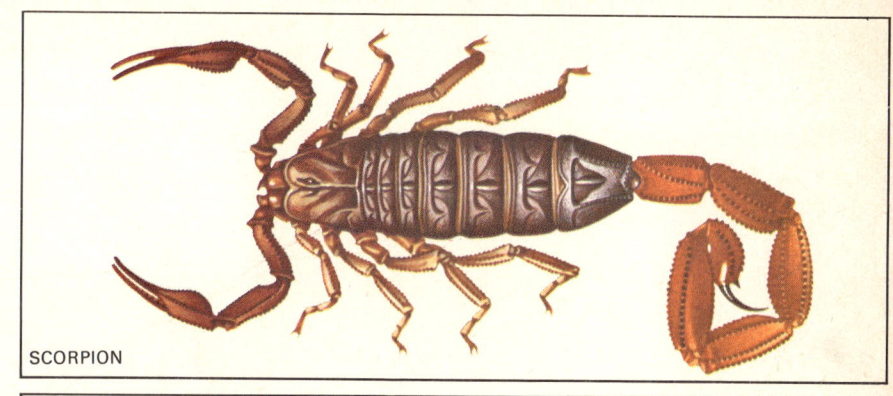

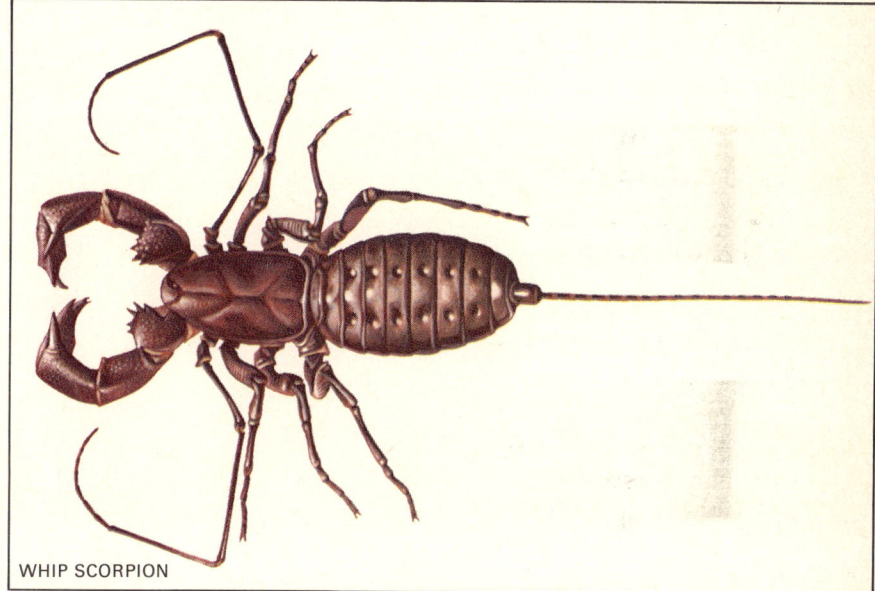

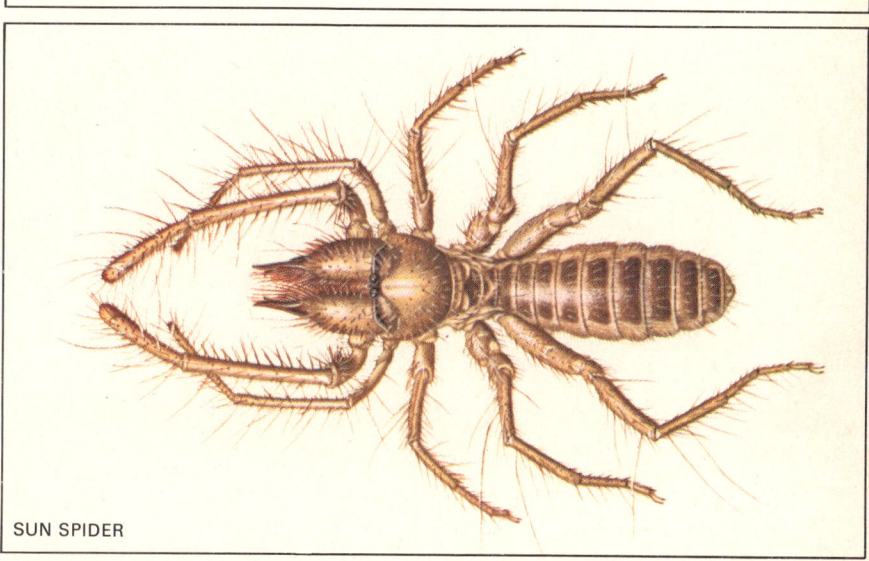

SCORPION

WHIP SCORPION

SUN SPIDER

all at once. Many a roadrunner has been seen walking around for a whole day with a snake hanging out of its mouth, swallowing another inch or two from time to time as the lower end is digested.

Probably the bird most associated with the desert is the evil-looking vulture. These birds are common but harmless. They are so weak that they cannot kill animals and eat only dead meat. Their excellent eyesight enables them to spot other hovering vultures at great distances; if they see a fellow bird descend toward a likely source of food they will follow, giving a sign for still other vultures—even farther off—to head their way. Sometimes the vultures will hover over a weakening animal, watching it patiently until it dies.

One of the largest groups of animals on the desert are the mammals. By far the majority are seedeaters, and the enormous supply of seeds in the desert supplies a large mammal population, primarily rodents.

In addition there are some browsing species, such as deer, antelope and rabbits, which live on foliage and twigs as well as on water-storing plants such as the cactus. Foxes, jackals, badgers, big cats and skunks are carnivores that eat other animals. And bats, shrews and a few moles subsist on insects.

From kit foxes *(page 50)* to shrews, the desert mammals tend to be paler in color than the other species of their families, which live in humid, well-vegetated places. For a long time scientists assumed that the reason

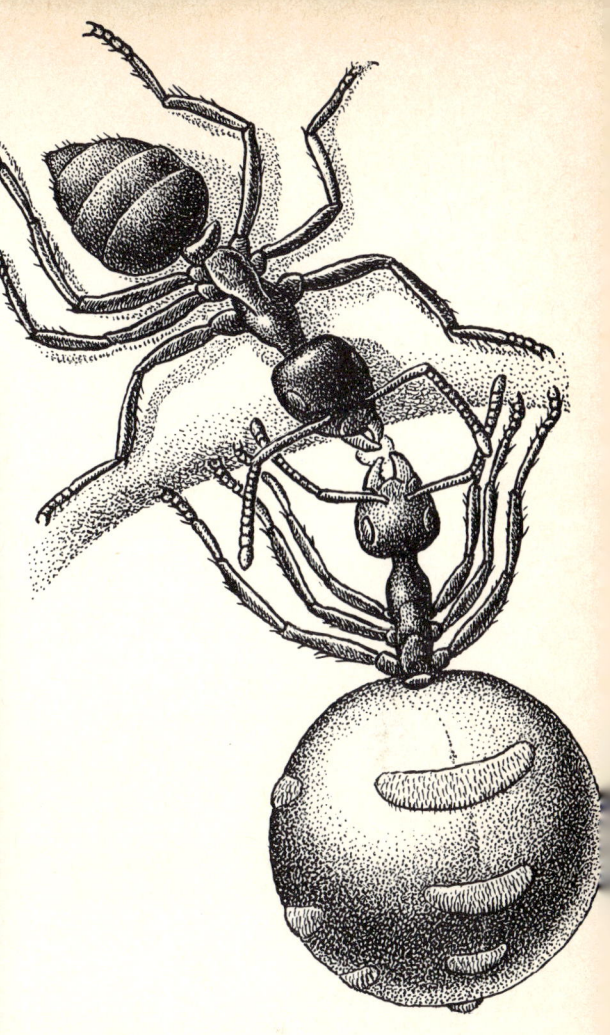

Sweet Storage Tanks

Glistening like golden Christmas ornaments, swollen honeypot ants hang from the roof of their nest *(left)*. Honeypots are young ants chosen to hoard nectar. When food is plentiful in the desert, worker ants pump sweet juices into the honeypots *(above)*, whose bodies expand and store the nectar until it is needed.

for their paleness was the result of natural selection to camouflage them against the pale background colors of the desert. But this may not be the whole reason. The question has been raised whether their paleness might not actually be a discoloration caused by the hot, dry air, for paleness would seem to offer no particular advantage to many species that only come out at night, like bats, or underground animals, like moles. So far the cause of paleness remains one of the desert's many mysteries.

Beyond mere paleness, there are certain kinds of coloration that could be produced only by selective evolution. The mottled browns and grays of the horned lizard blend perfectly into stretches of the desert's pebbly ground. So does the coloration of the poorwill, which sits all day cuddled among the rocks. In New Mexico's Tularosa Basin, Seth B. Benson described the case of two neighboring groups of pocket mice: one, living on a black lava flow, was black and the other, living in the sand dunes, was nearly white. Selective evolution must be the cause; such close matching of background color has enormous protective value to the animals that use it to hide themselves from the sight of their enemies.

The mammals' most important protection comes, naturally, from the burrows that undermine the desert like the tangle of service tunnels under a great city. Earth is an admirable insulator against heat and aridity, and an animal taking its ease a few inches below the surface may comfortably survive the hottest day and the coldest night. A study of gerbil burrow systems on the Kara Kum Desert of the Soviet Union showed a difference of 31° between the ground surface at midday and a point only four inches underground. Even more dramatically, when the sands of the Mojave reach 150°, a burrow 18 inches below the surface will register a cool 61°. Down in a burrow the humidity is relatively high, too, which helps an animal reduce its water loss. Finally, the burrow serves the burrower as a safe retreat from most of its natural enemies, though not from snakes.

Burrowing rodents gather seeds when they fall to the ground and store them in caches for use during the lean periods of drought or cold. W. T. Shaw found that the giant kangaroo rat of the southern San Joaquin Valley in California made temporary shallow caches of seeds during the harvest season and then at leisure gathered and moved these stores to permanent granaries in the main burrow.

Around the burrow of one rat, Shaw located 875 temporary caches in an area of five square yards. Some of the seeds, marked with Mercurochrome, were recovered later from the rat's main underground storehouse. In southern Arizona another student, Hudson Reynolds, found that Merriam kangaroo rats removed marked seeds from feeding stations and buried them in caches at an average distance of 50 feet from the source. Later the rats dug up most, but not all, of the seeds, for some of the caches produced clus-

The Day It Rained Shrimp

Brought to life by a heavy desert storm, newly hatched fresh-water shrimp cover the bed of a dry lake (*above*) after 25 years as unhatched eggs. Long ago, before the lake dried, shrimp thrived in it. As the water dwindled, shrimp eggs adapted by lying dormant in the mud between infrequent rains. Scientists like the man digging for eggs (*left*) believe the eggs can survive encased in mud for a century.

ters of plant seedlings after heavy rains. In this way, among many others, rodents scatter seeds and help the spread of plants.

Each continent of the world has a few unique animal species, but on the whole, the forces of evolution have cast desert animals the world over in similar molds. If all the vertebrate animals from the deserts of North and South America, Asia, Africa, and Australia could be assembled in one spot, those from any one continent would look amazingly like those from any other—with the exception of the Australian contingent. And even though Australian marsupials—or pouch-bearing mammals—do not look like other animals, they have very similar adaptations.

One example of similar adaptation is supplied by a group of small rodents found on every major desert in the world. One description fits them all, though they have evolved from very different species. These animals—small ratlike rodents that look like tiny kangaroos—have long, powerful hind legs and tiny front ones. They move by jumping and have long tufted tails to balance them. Large hearing chambers in their skulls amplify sounds of the nearly silent desert. Apparently animals of this description are so perfectly fitted for desert life that evolution has produced them over and over again. In America there is the kangaroo rat, in Africa the gerbil, in the Middle East the jerboa. Even in Australia the type is represented by a marsupial kangaroo rat.

The American kangaroo rat, like all of its look-alikes, has astonishing speed and needs it, for it is the basic food of many desert predators. Pursued by a kit fox or a coyote, a kangaroo rat can cover 20 feet per second in two-foot hops. Its tail helps it to zigzag, and it can make right-angle turns in mid-jump. What makes it a prized dish for other desert dwellers is that its body is 65 per cent water even though it may never drink a drop. Instead it manufactures water from its food.

Desert creatures are amazingly abundant, wonderfully varied examples of how well some animal life can adapt itself to unbelievably harsh conditions. Many desert animals are so perfectly suited to their arid environment that they would quickly die if they were moved to a gentler climate.

Death on the Arid Sands

Baking under an intense sun, the grotesque skeleton of a giraffe sprawls across a desolate African desert. The animal was a victim of a prolonged drought. Normally, giraffes survive rainless periods by feeding on drought-resistant plants. But during an extended dry spell, even these hardy creatures may perish.

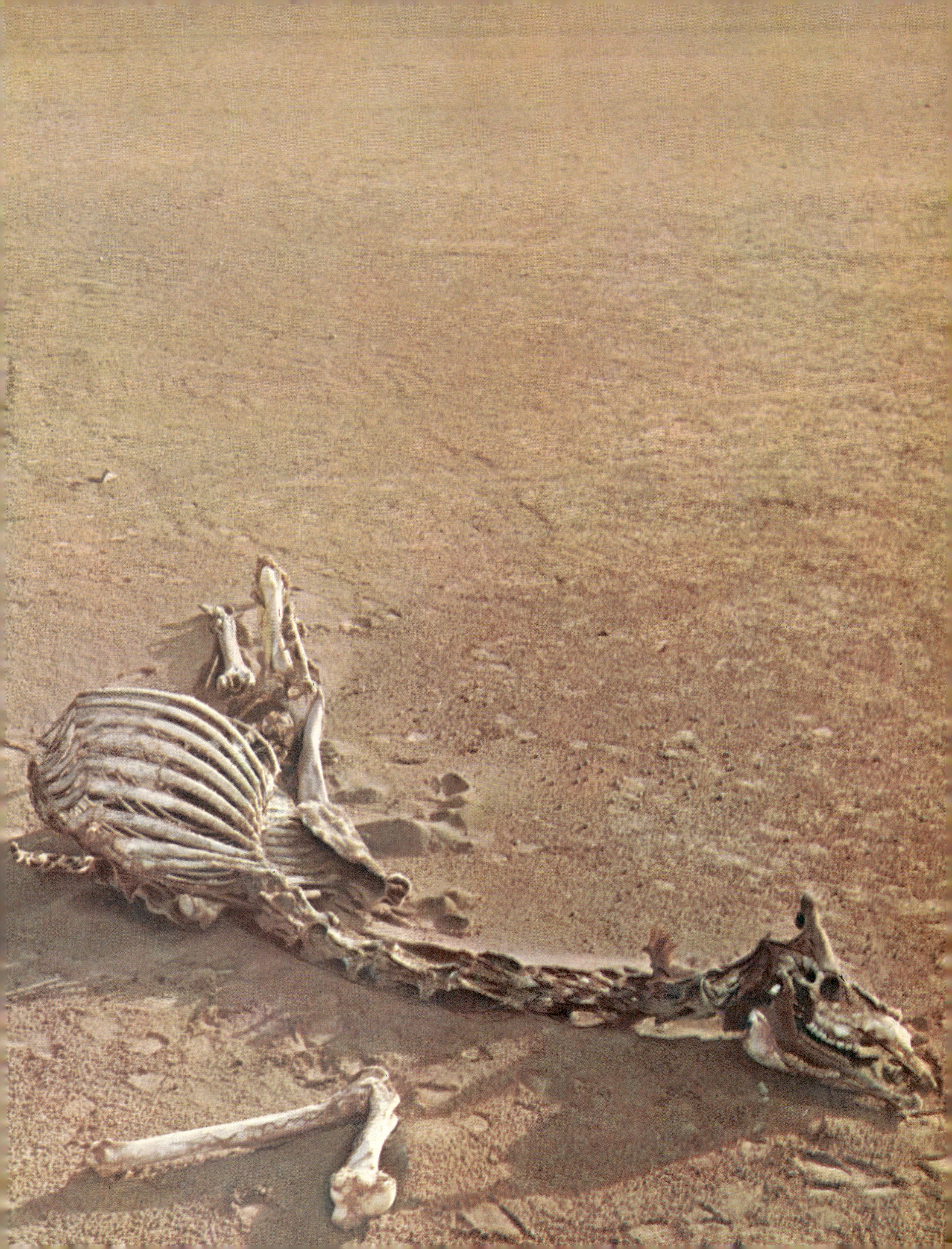

CAREFULLY AVOIDING the sharp spines, a pack rat nibbles on a prickly pear. In the desert, green plants are the starting point of a food chain, for they serve as the main source of food and moisture to animals such as the pack rat. These plant-eating animals are in turn the prey of meat eaters.

5
Staying Alive in the Desert

The question of how desert animals manage to survive interested even the earliest naturalists. Because it is so hot, these animals need a great deal of water to cool themselves, but the desert is the last place on earth to look for a great deal of water. Modern scientists who study desert animals are beginning to find that these animals have a great variety of very clever ways of coping with their most severe problem—conserving their precious supply of water.

One rather unexpected discovery is that desert animals cannot stand heat much better than their relatives who live in cooler and moister climates. Desert animals show severe symptoms of distress—similar to those of a human with a high fever—whenever their internal temperature is forced much higher than normal. On deserts where the temperature in the shade often exceeds 120° F. (and on the sunlit ground, 150°), every animal must have a way of beating the heat. Most amphibians, reptiles and smaller mammals solve the problem by just going underground where temperatures are lower. But there are many that cannot retreat into burrows and must cool themselves in other ways.

Almost all animals, including man, cool themselves mainly by ridding themselves of water in a process called evaporation, for when water evaporates, it releases the heat it has gained as it passed through the body. The methods of evaporation vary among different animal groups. But basically there are three places where the body may expose water to evaporation for cooling: in the lungs during breathing, in the mouth where water appears in the form of saliva and on the skin as perspiration or sweat. But not every animal uses all three of these cooling devices. Reptiles and birds depend almost entirely on their lungs for cooling; that is, they pant when they get hot, and their moist breath releases water. Some mammals, like the fox, the coyote and others also rely on panting. Some of the marsupials of Australia, like the koala and the wallaby, begin to produce saliva freely as the temperature rises, and they spread the liquid over their bodies with their tongues. The desert wallaby, a smaller relative of the kangaroo, both pants and salivates, licking its whole body with saliva and also rubbing its face with wet paws.

For man, sweating is, of course, the most important cooling system. It is even better developed in the horse and some other large hoofed animals. Many other mammals have sweat glands, although these glands are relatively few in number. In some animals evaporation may take place directly from the skin even though there are no signs of sweating. For an animal of a given weight, the larger the area of exposed skin, the more water can be evaporated for cooling. It is quite likely that the large ears of the jack rabbit, with their networks of blood vessels, are as important for cooling as for hearing, since they expose so much skin to evaporation.

Body cooling is very complicated for the hoofed animals that have a compound stomach, in which food is held for partial digestion by bacteria. For example, in summer the desert mule deer eats mostly twigs and leathery leaves of various shrubs, which is the best forage available. This diet is high in cellulose, which is hard to digest and would have little food value to the deer except for the fact that the bacteria in the stomach partially digest the cellulose. This arrangement is of advantage to the deer, but it also creates a problem because a great amount of heat is generated by the bacteria in the process of digestion. The deer gets rid of some of the heat by belching. But getting rid of stomach heat puts an added strain on the cooling system of the deer's body, for it increases the animal's water requirement. In cold weather there is no problem; in fact, the stomach heater becomes an advantage.

Besides the water needed for cooling, some must be used in eliminating waste products from the body. Animals that have ample supplies of water use it freely in urine and solid wastes, but desert animals have had to reduce this water loss to a bare minimum. The problem is fairly simple in reptiles and birds, for their kidneys remove poisonous nitrogen

Give and Take

High up in a saguaro cactus, an elf owl peeks out of its nest. This is a fine example of how animals and plants live together in the desert. The owl, seeking a shelter, has moved into an abandoned Gila woodpecker nest. The cactus, meanwhile, has produced a shell around the cavity to prevent the loss of its precious water supply.

74

containing waste from the blood in the form of uric acid; this acid is easily concentrated and therefore can be excreted in a small quantity of water. But mammals have a different chemical system of purification, which yields urea. Since urea is not so readily concentrated, getting rid of it requires a good deal of water.

Meat- and insect-eating mammals, whose diet is high in protein, use much more water for excretion than do the vegetarian mammals, whose intake is primarily sugars and starches. This is because the waste product of protein is the main component of urea. And if urea is allowed to accumulate, it becomes highly poisonous in the body. For this reason, the insect-eating bats must drink water daily, even though they take in a great deal of water with the protein-rich bodies of the insects they devour.

The seeds eaten by rodents contain far less water than do the insects eaten by bats; seed-eating rodents can get along without additional drinking water because their diet is low in protein and their need to dispose of urea is much less.

To supply the water required for cooling and excretion, animals have a third primary source besides drinking water and the water present in their food. This is the water produced chemically as a by-product of food digestion.

The camel has an ancient and deserved reputation for going without drinking water for very long periods. For a long time it was

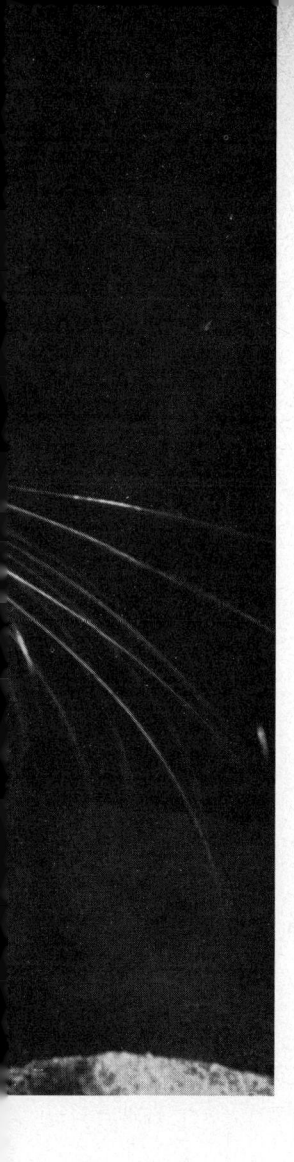

Unrelated Look-Alikes

Though similar in appearance, the dwarf kangaroo rat (*above*) of the American desert and the jerboa (*opposite*) of Africa and Asia are not related. Their resemblance is a case of convergent evolution—similar development because of similar environments. Both eat plants and dry seeds; both escape enemies by rapid leaps on oversized hind legs. Both have long tails that help them in leaping and turning.

thought that the camel's hump was really a water reservoir. But now scientists know that the camel's hump is not a water storage device, although it does play an important role in keeping the camel supplied with water. It works like this: when green vegetation is available, camels can live for months without drinking at all, for they get all the water they need in their food. But during the Saharan summer there is little greenery in the desert for the camels to feed on. The dried-up grasses contain virtually no moisture.

The camel's hump is filled largely with fat, accumulated when food and water are available; when other food is not available, this fat is digested. During digestion, hydrogen is released, and combines with the oxygen breathed in by the camel to produce water.

When water is available again, the animal will drink as much (say 25 gallons) as it lost. However, it takes a little time for the water to be returned to tissues throughout the body. The hump gradually swells to normal size after the camel is back on an adequate diet.

The little kangaroo rat has worked out its needs for water with a method quite different from the camel's. During the dry season there is rarely any chance for a kangaroo rat to drink ordinary water or even to sip the dew from leaves or grass. Therefore it depends mostly on its diet of dry seeds and occasional nibbles of vegetation for its water. Seeds contain scant amounts of water (about 4 per cent), to which is added the water pro-

HUMP FAT USED UP

HUMP FAT RESTORED

Flexible Storage Space

Thirsty camels crowd a drinking trough *(left)*. These animals can live in the desert for long periods without food or water, drawing energy from fat stored in their humps. During shortages, the hump dwindles *(top)* as the camel burns up the fat and produces water as a by-product. When food and water are available again, the hump gradually returns to its normal size.

A Story on the Desert Floor

This aerial view of a dry lake (*right*), resembling an abstract painting, helps explain how the jack rabbit (*left*) survives in the desert's unfriendly atmosphere. The white splotches are high ground, on which mesquite grows. The thin solid lines are rabbit tracks, while the dotted lines are tracks made by cattle. As the cattle overgraze the land, grasses die and mesquite thrives. Cattle will not eat mesquite, but it is a favorite food of the rabbits. So, rabbits flourish and fewer cattle find forage.

duced by digestion. Under normal circumstances this amount of water is just barely sufficient to meet the modest living requirements of the animal.

Even so, the animal lives a precarious life, and all of its water-saving efforts can be defeated by a change in weather conditions. This is because the balance of water intake and output is strongly affected by the humidity of the air: the drier the air, the more moisture is lost in evaporation and the less is taken in with the seeds.

Desert animals have another useful trick to escape heat: they fall into a deep sleep. All birds and mammals are considered to be "warm-blooded"—that is, they have built-in regulators to keep their body temperatures at or near a normal operating level. In man these devices are very precise, and unless we are ill or are taking part in strenuous exercise, we live our lives at a body temperature between 98° and 99°. But in wild animals there is a great deal more variation. Some animals whose body temperatures can fall far below normal are even able to hibernate, that is, they fall into a deep sleep, like a coma, known as dormancy. There are important advantages in dormancy. If the food supply is short, an animal can conserve energy and live much longer by lowering body temperature and thereby lowering the rate at which its body uses up food. This is especially true of very small animals. Because

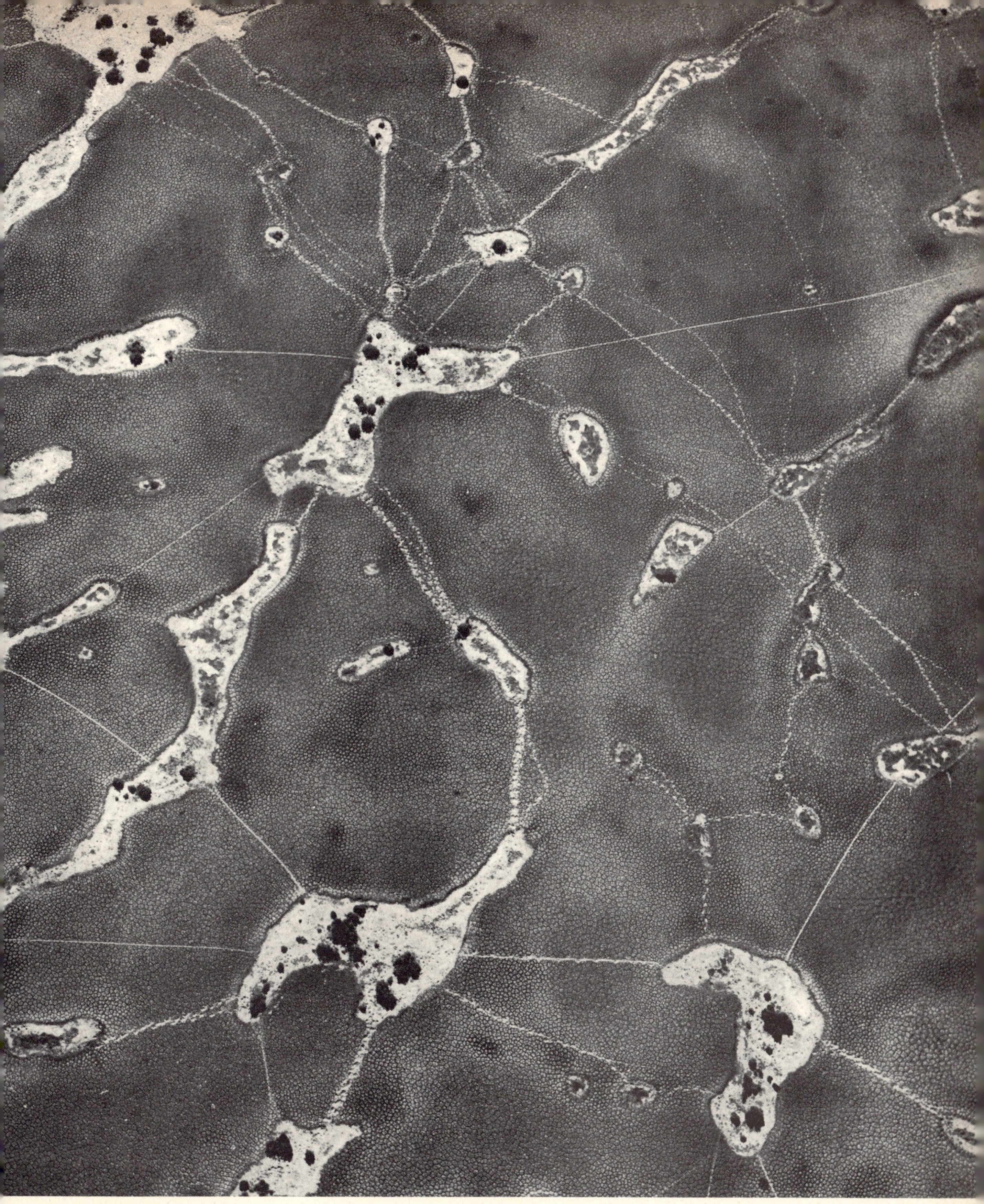

they are easily heated or cooled by their surroundings, they have to use relatively more energy to keep their body heat at an even level than do the larger animals. It is natural therefore to find that most hibernators are small in size.

The pocket mouse, one of the tiniest of desert rodents, is a hibernator about which desert students know a great deal. Called the pocket mouse for the seed-carrying pouches in its cheeks, it is a smaller edition of the kangaroo rat, and its general habits are similar. It stores seeds in its burrow, gets both food and water from them and goes about as far as possible in reducing its requirements of water. For example, it has absolutely no need to supplement the diet with water from green, moisture-laden vegetation. In times of extreme heat and drought or during periods of severe winter cold, the mouse gets no particular advantage from eating its hard-earned stores of seeds merely to stay awake. So it falls into a deep sleep, and its body temperature drops to slightly above that of the burrow. In summer the ground is fairly warm, so that sleep is not so profound or continuous as it is in winter.

This summer sleep is called estivation. The mouse drops into a fitful sleep, and its body temperature, which ranges from 91° to 102° while it is awake, drops to the neighborhood of 60° to 67°. During experiments, these mice go into estivation when they are given no food. When kept at a temperature of about 60°, the mice drowse for days, stirring only for short periods. But as the temperature is dropped to near freezing, the mice slip into deep hibernation, with a body temperature as low as 43°. At this point breathing

Tricks for Staying Alive

Two desert reptiles—the chuckwalla lizard (*left*) and the fringe-toed sand lizard (*above*)—demonstrate how they foil their enemies and survive. When threatened, the chuckwalla ducks into a handy crevice. There it gulps air and bloats its body, thus wedging itself so firmly in the rock that it cannot be moved. The sand lizard dives into loose sand to hide (*top*). Aided by toes designed for digging and a built-in sand filter in its nose to prevent choking, this lizard can quickly "swim" out of sight (*bottom*).

81

almost stops and the body "burns" almost no food at all. What little energy is consumed to maintain life comes from fat deposits stored in the body. This is the state in which pocket mice and other hibernators spend the cold winter months. Warm weather revives them, and when fully awake they emerge as good as new.

Some birds utilize this same procedure to save energy. Various species of swifts frequently nest on desert cliffs, and normally they hunt each day to catch the flying insects that are their whole bill of fare. But occasionally wind and rain ground their insect food for several days in a row, and the birds would probably starve if they maintained normal body temperature. Instead, both adults and nestlings become torpid, that is, they become sluggish and inactive. This change seems to take place as soon as there is a food shortage; the birds revive as soon as conditions improve and food again becomes available.

Poorwills and nighthawks are nocturnal insect-catching birds that are most at home in a desert habitat. They have just about the same food problem as the swifts, and they, too, become torpid for short periods. Moreover, in winter the poorwill apparently enters into deep hibernation.

In studying two California birds that visit the desert, the Allen and Anna hummingbirds, a scientist found that they become torpid every night, regardless of weather. Shortly after settling on the evening roost, these tiny birds fall asleep and then quickly advance into a dormant state, with temperature reduced to 12° or 15° below normal. In the morning their temperature rises to normal, and the birds go about their business of gathering nectar and insects.

Out of hard necessity, the animals of the desert have taken advantage of a wide variety of tricks to make ends meet in food and water needs. Yet—differing from the desert plants—not one of these "cheating" mechanisms is actually unique to desert animal species. Hibernation, for one thing, is very common among rodents throughout the world. Loss of water by evaporation is a universal cooling process. What is impressive about the strenuous adaptations made by the desert animals is the marvelous precision with which the mechanisms are combined in each species, so that life can go on with minimal supplies of water.

A Portable Water Supply

In search of plant food, a desert tortoise lumbers across a flat stretch. These reptiles have adapted well to the scarcity of water in the desert. They are able to convert some of their food into water and store it in sacs under their shells. A full supply—about a pint—can last through an entire dry season.

IN A TIMELESS SCENE, Bushmen cross the Kalahari Desert of Africa, as their ancestors once did, in search of game. They carry all that they own. Cut off from the modern world, Bushmen lead a primitive existence. Yet, their nomadic ways are successful, for they have lived in the desert for centuries.

6
Man against the Desert

Man was not cut out to live in the desert. If a healthy human adult is stranded in the middle of a desert, without water, on the morning of a hot summer day, he will feel no discomfort at first. But in an hour he will lose up to a quart of salty water by perspiring and will be very thirsty. By midafternoon, as his body tries its best to throw off heat by perspiring, his weight will drop 12 to 18 pounds and he will be weak. By nightfall, if it has been a 120° F. day, he may well be dead. But if the temperature has gone only to 110° in the shade, he can expect to live through one more such day before dying. Even if he had enough water to allow him a gallon a day instead of none at all, the sun would kill him within a week.

Nevertheless, as far back as human existence can be traced, men have found ways to

Africa

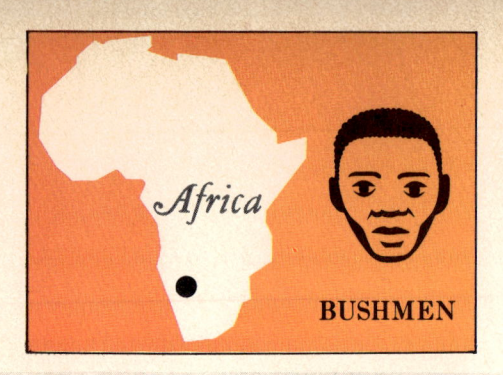

BUSHMEN

survive in desert lands. Unlike the camel, whose hump helps supply otherwise unavailable water, no race of men has ever evolved any important physical adaptation that would make life easier in the desert. Despite this failure every division of humanity is well represented among the regular inhabitants of the world's deserts. Negroid peoples have survived many centuries in all the deserts of Africa; Caucasoid, or European, peoples have lived successfully in both African and Middle Eastern deserts; so have Mongoloid peoples in the deserts of Asia and the Americas, and Australoid men in deserts the length and breadth of Australia.

Different groups have found very different ways of dealing with the desert's intense heat, particularly in the vital matter of what clothes they wear. The Bushmen of Africa and the aborigines of Australia go stark naked in the sun, or wear little patches of cloth or leather purely for decoration. Most tribes

A Short Time for Play

Hundreds of years ago, the Bushmen were driven into the hostile Kalahari Desert. They adjusted well to their new life, as shown by the sturdiness of their young. Bushmen are indulgent with children, but adult duties come early. When they reach seven, the boys playing on the dunes *(opposite)* will start serious training for lives as young hunters, like the one at left. At the same age, the little girl drinking water from an ostrich egg shell *(above)* will begin to take on campsite responsibilities.

87

of the Sahara, Arabian and Asian Deserts prefer to cover themselves with clothing in order to shield the body from heat and cold and to cut down on evaporation of needed water through the skin.

Since heavily pigmented skin gives some protection against the sun's burning rays, Negroes are better off in this respect than lightly pigmented Caucasians. Fair-skinned people, subject to sunburn, are at a disadvantage because burning destroys the working of the sweat glands. If they are careful to tan gradually and guard against overexposure, lightly pigmented people can live in reasonable comfort in the sun-baked lands. And it is also true that many members of Caucasian desert tribes have dark skin.

Regardless of racial background, the human body does make a few slight physical adjustments as it gets used to the desert. The sweat glands gradually increase their output (up to somewhat more than a quart per hour), and come to respond more quickly to heat. Both the sweat glands and the kidneys change their working to slow the rate at which salt is lost from the body. Blood circulation is increased in the surface vessels, which helps to cool the body.

Although these small adjustments are a great help in adapting to desert life, there is one important adjustment that the human body simply cannot make. It cannot cut down the amount of water it loses, and it cannot survive for long on a less-than-normal supply of water. During World War II

Making the Best of a Hostile Wasteland

A young boy learning to use the bow and arrow (*opposite*), a finely muscled hunter about to spear game (*below, left*) and a trio returning to camp with fresh meat (*below*) show the primitive hunting methods of the Bushmen. Armed with spears and arrows that can kill only at short distances and faced with the typical desert shortages of food, the Bushmen have nevertheless made a life in the Kalahari. Some three centuries ago, there were nearly a million Bushmen. But a long series of wars with Europeans and local enemies almost wiped them out —only a few thousand survived the flight to the Kalahari. In a remarkable adaptation, their numbers have climbed in recent years back to 55,000.

SAHARAN PLATEAU

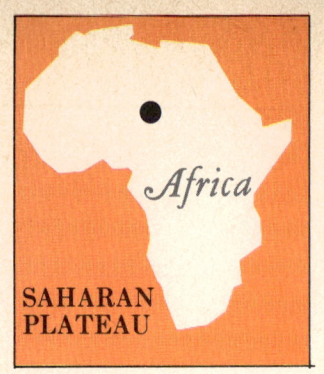

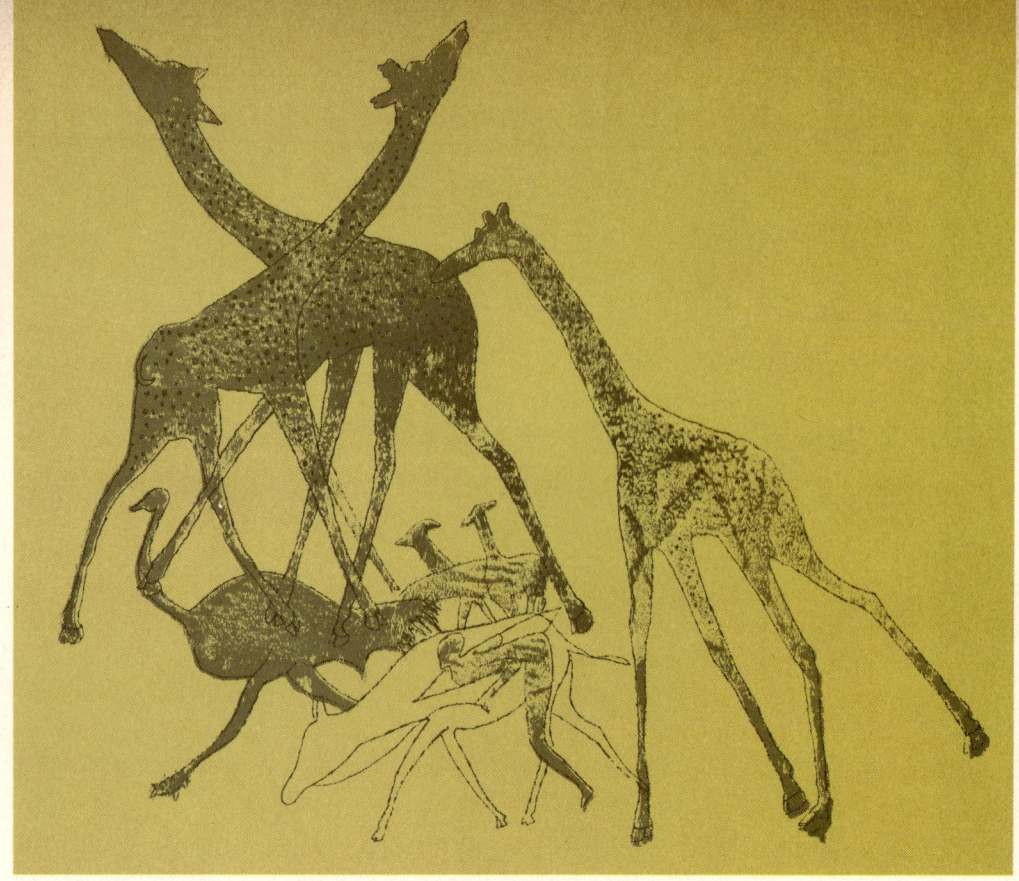

COW AND ARCHER

WILDLIFE

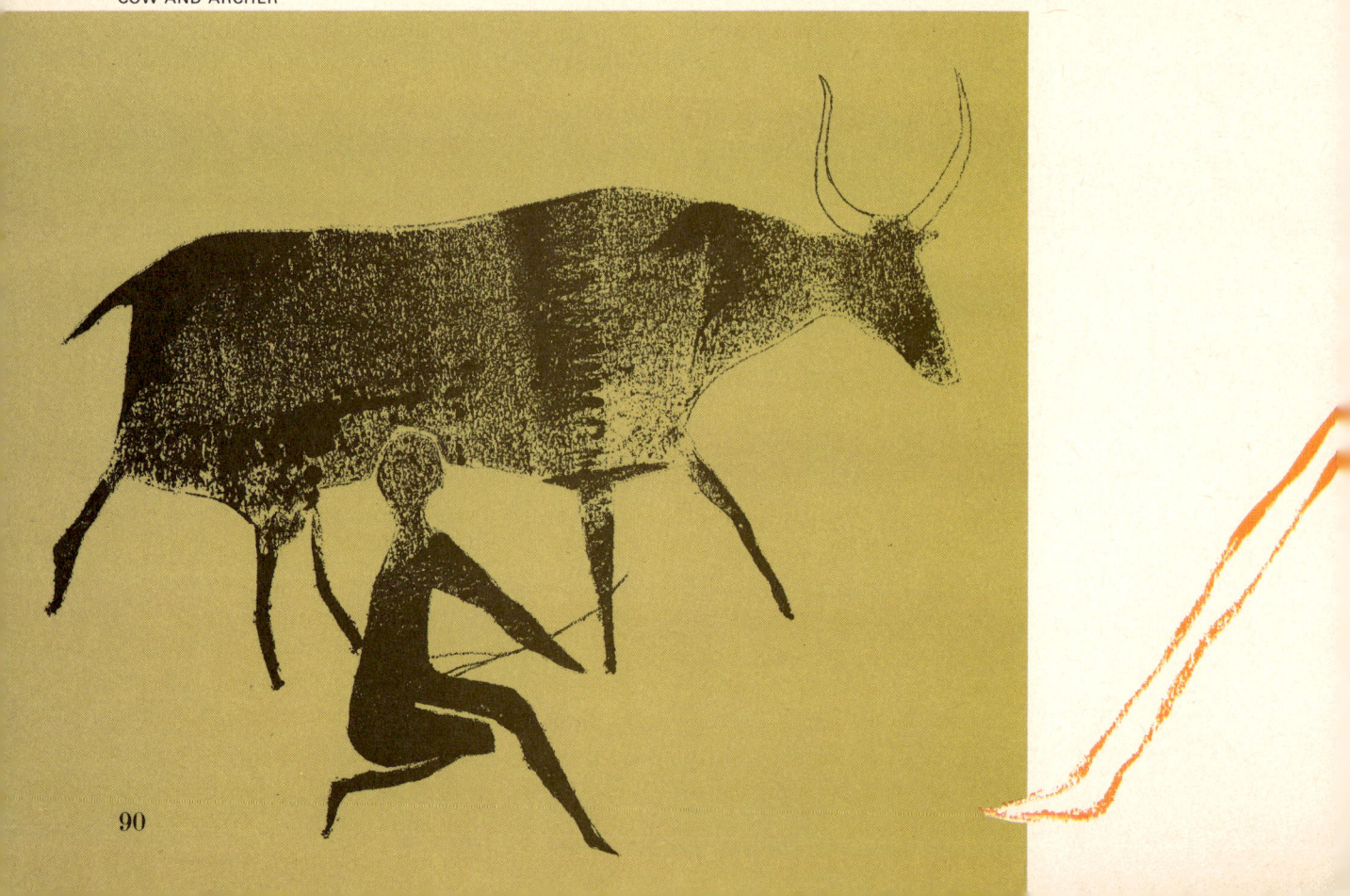

90

Once a Greener Land

Rock drawings found at Tassili-n-Ajjer in the Sahara show that this now-desolate plateau was once a green and fertile land. In those times enough grass grew to feed the giraffes, ostriches and antelopes pictured here. The drawing of the running man dates back 9,000 years. The cow and the archer were drawn by a member of a tribe that herded domestic animals in this area some 6,000 years ago.

RUNNING MAN

a group of scientists from the University of Rochester conducted elaborate studies of the water needs of American soldiers who were being trained in the Mojave Desert. They found that troops could be conditioned to withstand long marches and hard labor in the desert heat—so long as they had adequate drinking water. But cutting down the water intake quickly led to a breakdown of their physical controls over body temperatures, and heat prostration soon followed, even among men in excellent physical shape.

This is confirmed by experience in the Sahara where road-gang and oil-field workers get a daily allotment of two gallons of water per man for drinking and cooking alone; tests have shown that in a program of strenuous work, the body slowly weakens on anything less.

Some good survival advice for lost travelers in the desert has come from the researches of the Rochester team and others. Since dehydration, or drying out, is the greatest danger, reducing the possibility of water loss is the greatest goal to keep in mind. By walking only at night and sitting quietly in the shade during the day, both water loss and misery can be lessened. Wearing a full set of clothing may be uncomfortable during the daytime rest hours, but it slows evaporation. Resting places should be chosen out of the wind, in still air if possible. A cave is an ideal rest site, but clothing, piled rock or vegetation are good substitutes to give shade and wind protection.

People who stay with a broken-down automobile or crashed airplane have a better chance of being spotted in an air search than those who strike out cross-country. Every year, deserts claim the lives of people who, through panic or overconfidence, disregard this rule. A tragic example was provided by the crew of the American bomber *Lady Be Good*, which went far off course and crashed deep in the Sahara in 1943. The survivors mistook a line of hills to the north for the African coast, and headed that way. They walked by night and rested by day, and in a week actually covered 75 miles. But they were attempting more than the human system can stand: their bodies were found in 1960 where they had fallen, still 375 miles from the Mediterranean. As it happened, they would have died even if they had remained with their airplane, for it was not found until 1959, but the odds against them would have been a little less impossible. The Sahara abounds with tales of larger disasters overtaking even the most seasoned and des-

A Legend with a Basis in Fact

The familiar movie scene of heavily robed desert raiders swooping down on caravans is based in part on facts about the Tuareg. These Saharan people bundle up *(far right)* for protection against extreme heat and cold. For centuries, they lived partly on their pillage. When their raids were stopped by European settlers, the Tuareg turned into pastoral nomads *(right)*. Though no longer kidnappers, the Tuareg still keep slaves, like the young boy above, who are well treated and who perform menial jobs.

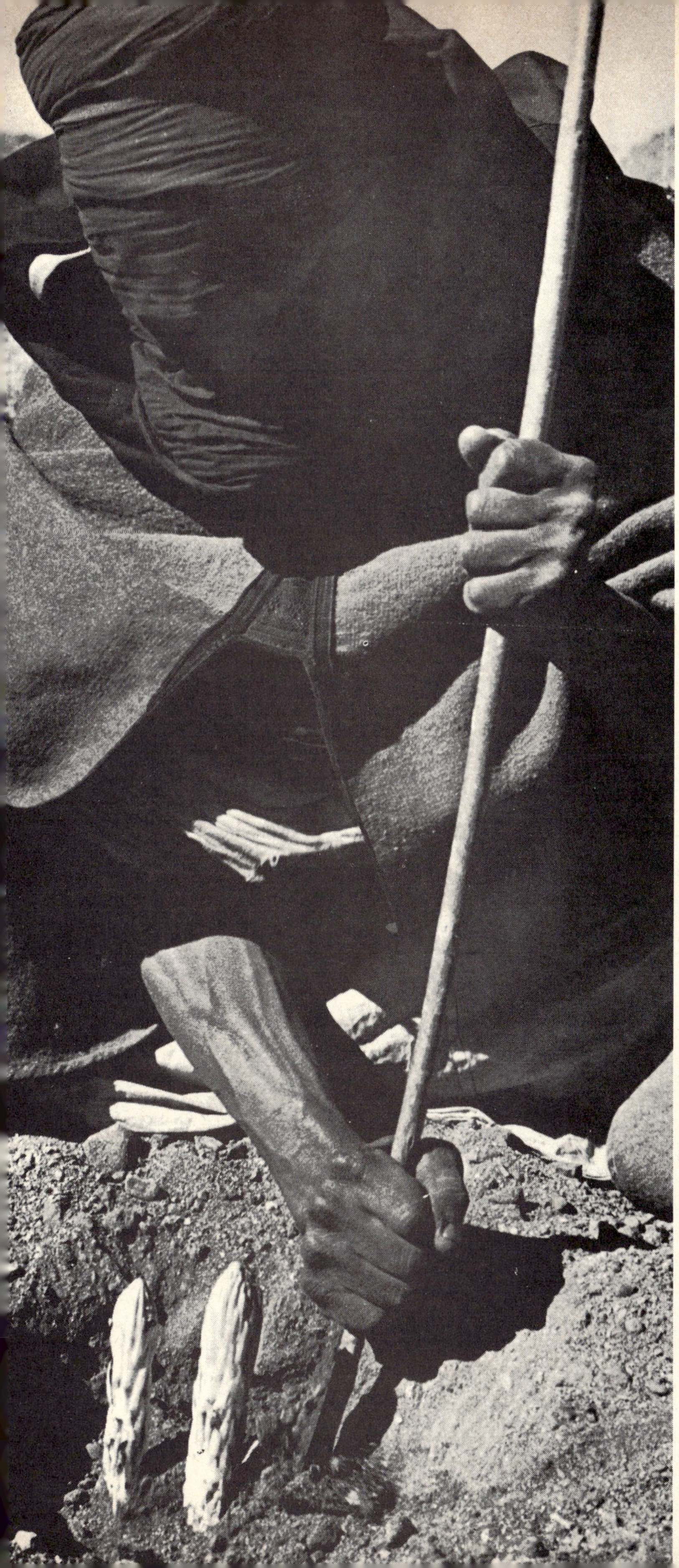
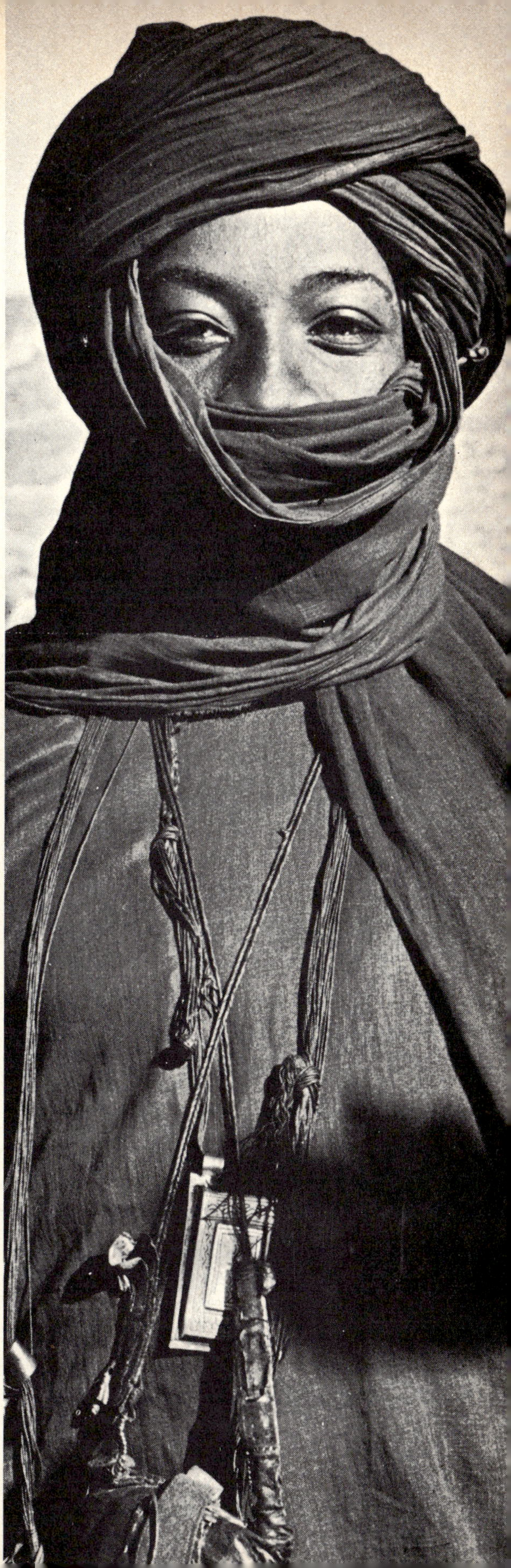

Africa

BERBERS

ert-wise wayfarers. In 1805, for example, an entire caravan of 2,000 men and 1,800 camels perished of thirst in the desert's south-central wastes, because water holes along their route had gone dry.

Most desert tribes are unaware of scientific strides on survival in the desert. They have come to terms with the heat and dryness of their land by a long process of trial and error. Among the most primitive of desert tribes—and probably as primitive as any people on earth—are the Bushmen of the Kalahari-Namib Desert region in Africa. They have never advanced beyond the Old Stone Age. These nomadic hunters and food gatherers plant no crops, have domesticated no animal but the dog and have no permanent houses. By avoiding activity whenever possible during the heat of the day, they can get along virtually without clothing. Probably because food is so hard to come by, children are not weaned until they are four or five. A child is carried on his mother's back or rides astride his father's shoulders and is always much plumper than his elders.

The Bushmen travel in small bands of several families, which share food and water. Each band "owns" a clearly defined territory, but may hunt outside it. When a band makes camp, each family clears a small patch of grass under a thorn tree, digs a shallow pit, called a *sherm*, big enough for all of them to sleep around a fire, and settles down until the next move. Several families may share the shade of one tree, their few belongings hanging from the branches. On cold nights the whole family huddles together by its fire, and it is the fire, rather than the *sherm*, that they regard as home.

The Bushmen forage for food in the cool early morning or at dusk. The women dig with sticks for edible roots and tubers and gather *tsama* melons, which have some food value but are prized mainly as a source of water during drought. They also stow water in empty ostrich-egg shells carried by the women. The men hunt antelope and smaller game with bows that shoot poison-tipped arrows, but when hunting is poor they help the women gather plant foods.

The wiry Bushman must have great endurance. Elizabeth Marshall Thomas, who lived among these people for two years, tells how a hunter may have to trot for four days after

Bundling Up to Stay Cool

A robed shepherd tends his flock on a North African range. While the shepherd's garment would seem to make him too warm for comfort, it actually protects him. The robe prevents direct sun and wind from reaching his body. Thus, perspiration evaporates more slowly—keeping the shepherd cooler.

Linked by a Desert Prophet

Seated on elaborate rugs, Arab women wait to pray. They are followers of Islam, the religion founded by Muhammad in the Seventh Century, after he saw visions in the desert. Religion is a major tie that links 110 million Arabs, whose world stretches across the dry lands from Morocco to the Persian Gulf.

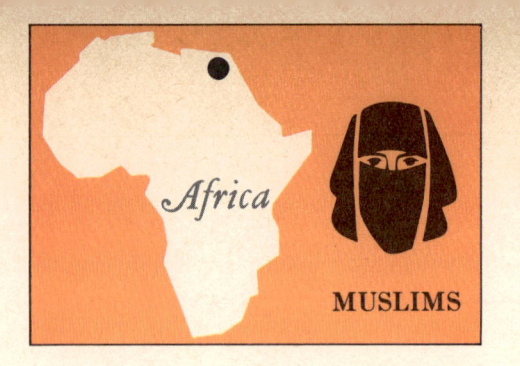

Africa

MUSLIMS

an antelope he has wounded, for the animal may wander 100 miles before it drops. The Bushman is so marvelously observant that he can recognize the tracks of the animal he has wounded from all others of its kind. Even a Bushman child walking along in the veld can tell his mother's footprints, can see at once the tiniest dry stalk among the grass that marks an edible root, or see a scorpion hidden in the dust and jump over it.

The Bushmen lack neither intelligence nor imagination. Their family life and religious beliefs are as intricate as they are among most groups of civilized people. But Bush-

Australia ABORIGINES

Stone Age Survivors

After a day of hunting, a family of Australian aborigines *(left)* rests on a rocky slope. Possessing only a few simple tools, these primitive people have survived in the desert for 25,000 years. Some tribes do not even have containers for water, and depend on puddles of rain water *(below)*, which they lap up on all fours. Today, as civilization approaches, the government has begun programs of education for these nomads.

men do lack nearly everything else that more advanced societies consider necessary to life. Above all, they lack communication with the outside world; they have no beasts of burden to extend their mobility beyond the distance a man can travel on foot.

Thanks to the horse and the camel, the donkey and the burro, the llama and the yak, the nomads—or wandering peoples—of other deserts have an economy based on livestock rather than hunting and gathering. They conduct trade with other peoples and pick up new ideas and skills by this civilizing contact. Their food supply is assured, they ride instead of walking while herding their stock, and they can take a few trappings of comfortable living along when they travel. The Mongols of the Gobi ride horses to herd their yaks and live in portable, roomy yurts made of felt stretched over collapsible willow frames. The Bedouin tent of woven goat hair stretched over lightweight poles is first of all a sunshade, second a shelter from wind and sand. A camel carries it with ease.

The nomadic herdsmen would not dream of roaming the desert as scantily clad as the

North America

SOUTHWEST INDIANS

Bushmen. They are heavily covered up, for good reason: riding and livestock herding require exposure to sun and wind throughout the day.

Desert agricultural tribes, while not nudists, wear much lighter clothing. They work in their fields during the day's cooler hours and have less need to protect their bodies from the sun. Since they have the food security of crops as well as animals, the soil-tilling tribes can give up wandering and live in permanent homes. The Pueblo Indians of the American Southwest made an art of the construction of thick-walled adobe houses; some of their structures have stood since prehistoric times.

Of all the deserts, the Sahara supports the most complex assortment of cultures. It is also strewn with the bones of earlier civilizations. For though in Arabic the desert's name means "brown and empty," the place has not always been so. From 60,000 to 6000 B.C. it was wet. Many of the river beds, now dust dry, ran full, and some of the vast plains, now so barren, were covered with forests that surged with life. Tribesmen pastured cattle on fertile fields and left vivid rock paintings that tell of their way of life (*pages 90-91*).

Gradually the area dried up and many of the flourishing tribes migrated or moved out. Today the desert is a terribly inhospitable place, but it is still home to three and a half million people, most of whom live in desperate squalor.

Among the tribes that still live there are the Tuareg, who, until 1902 when they were pacified by the French, were such fierce warriors that their territory became known as "the land of thirst and fear." Armed with sharp lances, antelope-hide shields and great swords, the Tuareg rode out on swift racing camels to prey on caravans and on oases controlled by other tribes. They added to their living by collecting four fifths of the crops grown by slaves at the Tuareg's own oases. After being subdued, they gave the French loyalty in exchange for food and protection.

Nowadays the Tuareg conduct a dwindling caravan trade, selling salt cakes to the cattle raisers of Black Africa. Since the Tuareg resist education, the sons of their ex-slaves outstrip Tuareg youth in school and

Sun-dried Food That Lasts

Hanging melons he has peeled and hollowed, an Indian of the American Southwest uses an ancient method of preserving food. When the melons dry, they will be stored. Most tribes in this desert were not nomads. Often settling on a riverbank, they built lasting homes, farmed and tended livestock.

go on to get better jobs. The Tuareg are riddled with disease, but statistics are lacking because the tribesmen also resist medical examination and treatment. Government authorities hope the Tuareg may have some future as a tourist attraction in their mountains, after the fashion of some American Indian reservation dwellers. As futures go (and as the Indian could testify), this would be a dismal one.

Another desert tribe is the Teda, some of whose members live in caves and rock shelters or in stone huts. They are divided into thousands of tiny clans and subtribes, as small as one family. They have kept their antique way of life, including even a moral code that all outsiders find perplexing. A young Teda suitor must prove his eligibility for marriage by stealing camels from another clan, yet camel stealing is regarded as a crime on a par with murder—which is perhaps equally common. Such a theft can touch off a feud that may last half a century, and hundreds of Teda have died as a result of a single camel theft.

The proudest and traditionally the richest tribe of the desert is the Reguibat of the west, Africa's greatest camel traders. Contemptuous of frontiers, they are accustomed to roaming freely across the borders of Morocco, Mauritania and the Sahara proper. Once these hawk-nosed, fanatical Muslim warriors dominated the desert as far down as Timbuktu, as well as Morocco and Spain. In the past few years they have fallen on

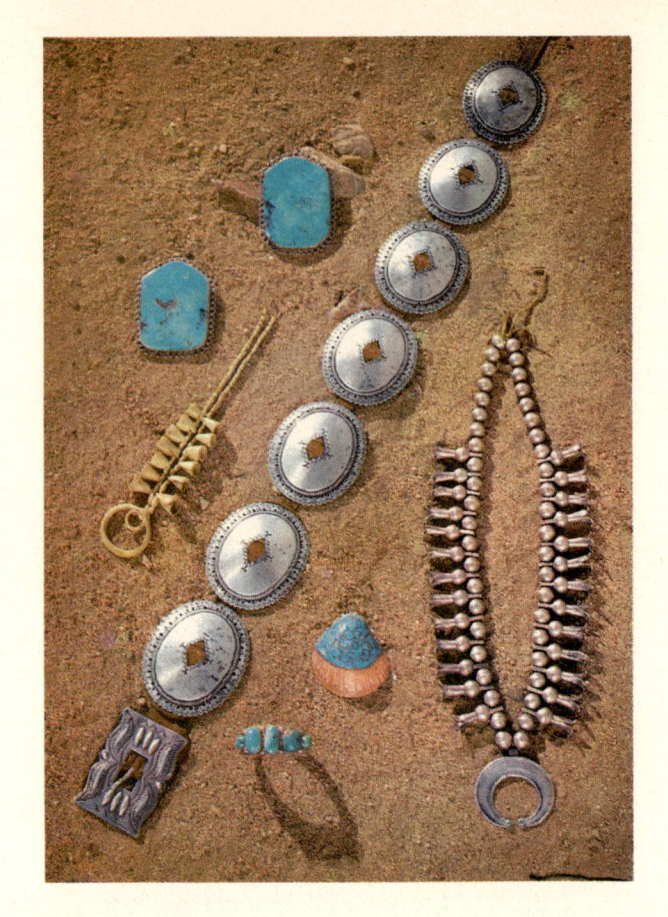

Elaborate Works of Artisans

Many Indian tribes of the American Southwest have traditionally shown a flair for intricate arts. The 12 pieces of pottery (*right*) were shaped by artists of many different tribes; the Navaho jewelry (*above*) displays a highly skilled ability to work with materials as different as silver and turquoise. Other artistic creations produced by various tribes included elaborately woven rugs and colorful sand paintings.

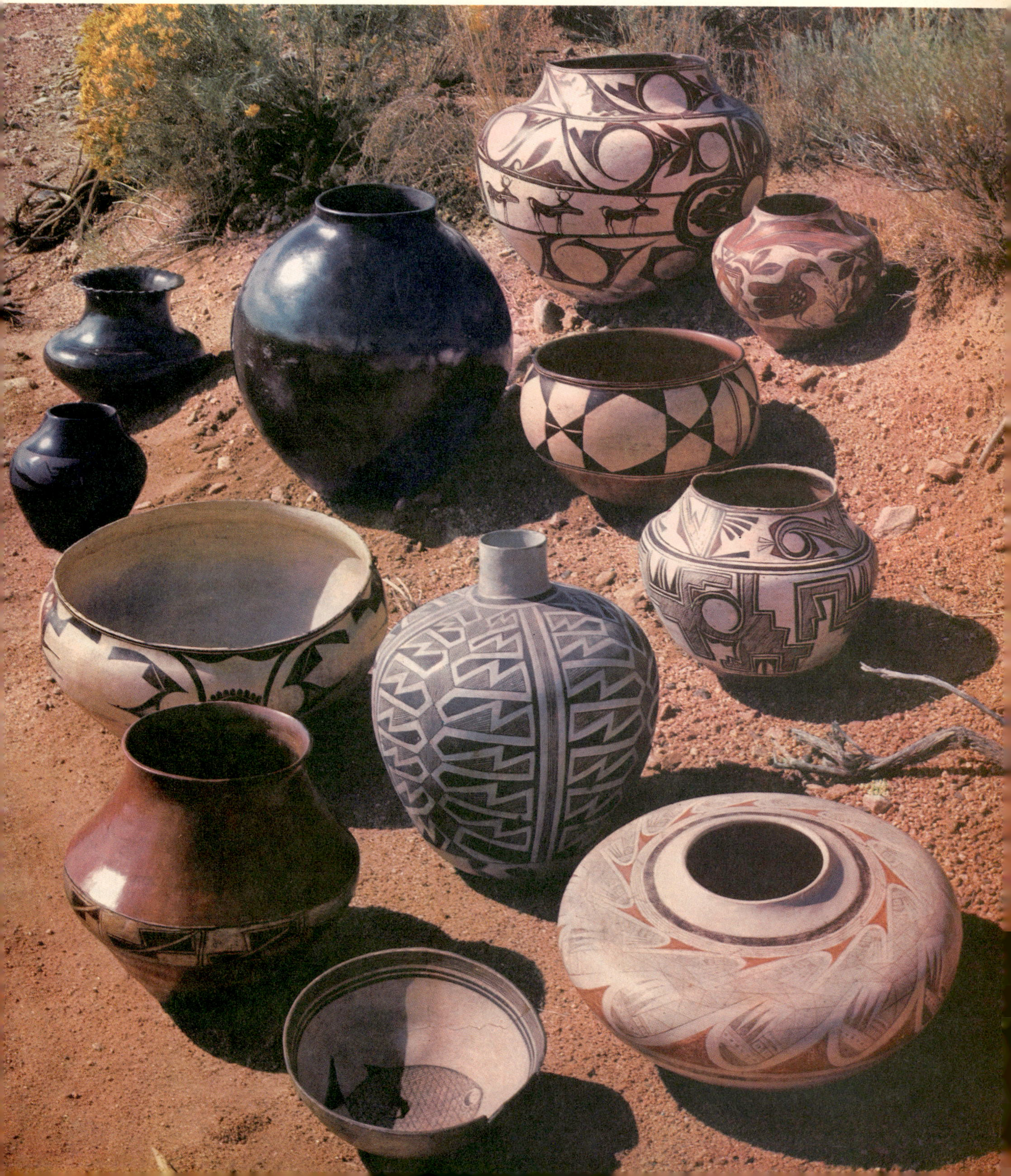

Houses Built to Last

Constructed 300 years ago, a pueblo on top of an Arizona mesa sits beneath a baking sun. Pueblos, built of dried mud, housed entire communities; when more space was needed, rooms were added. One five-story structure in New Mexico had 800 rooms and sheltered over 1,000 people.

hard times. They used to make their living by selling camels—some 15,000 or more every year—at Africa's biggest camel fair at Goulimine, in southern Morocco. But widespread use of the camel has declined in the increasingly motorized Sahara, and a few years ago Moroccan authorities, in a quarrel with the lawless Reguibat, banned the fair.

More aware than most nomadic tribes, the Chamba of the northwestern central Sahara have adapted to 20th Century change and even benefited from it. For years these Arabs provided the manpower for the "Meharistes," the French camel-corps police force. Like the Sikh in India, the Chamba tends to drift into employment that puts him on the side of law and order. Today Chamba are in the administration and are settling down in the oases as merchants and farmers and also taking jobs in the oil fields.

For nine centuries the Mozabites have inhabited the northern Sahara desert hollows where, occasionally, the river Mzab flows (its bed is dry for as long as seven years in a row). The valley became their last refuge in a period when they were pursued and persecuted by other Muslims for their views (they do not believe that Muhammad wrote all of the books for which he is given credit). Their "tribe" numbers about 40,000 today and is as wealthy as the Moors used to be. They owe their prosperity to the fact that they were forced, from the time they settled in their valley, to seek their fortunes outside its boundaries.

They became the shopkeepers of coastal Algeria. To orthodox Muslims, trade was distasteful, but the Mozabites did not share this prejudice. They operate shops by the hundreds in the cities of Algeria, in Morocco and Tunisia, and all the way down to Black Africa, and are big real-estate holders. They are the most skillful masons, carpenters and gardeners of all the desert dwellers. Every Mozabite who can afford one—and there are few poor Mozabites—has his carefully cultivated garden plot—and sends his surplus onions, carrots and tomatoes to be sold in the market place.

Even the richest Mozabites meekly give in to the austere dictates of the *halga*, the ironhanded council of religious elders who run the community. The council frowns on show and vulgar display of wealth, and until lately no Mozabite was permitted to have a telephone. A few younger ones have introduced refrigerators, washing machines and bright colors into their modest homes; but the neighbors contemptuously refer to these modernized dwellings as "Picasso houses."

The elders force adherence to the customs that make the Mozabites the strictest sect

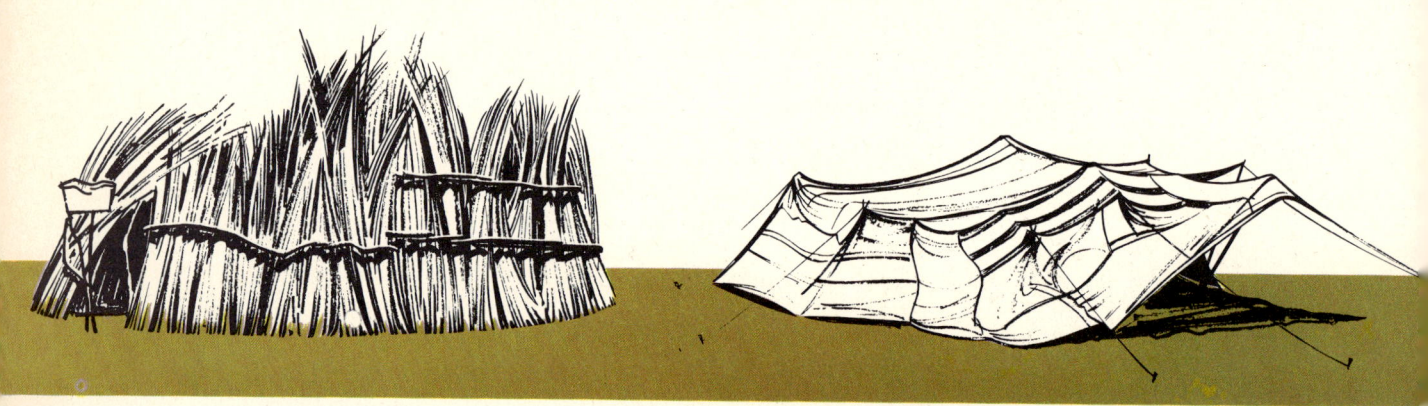

TUAREG ZERIBA

BEDOUIN TENT

in the Arab world. Parents still choose a son's bride—when she is about 10—and once she is "promised" she goes to live with her future husband's family and becomes a veiled, lifelong prisoner. Except to visit a family grave, Mozabite women rarely set foot outside their homes. Some of the husbands are aware of the oddity that permits them to learn French, go into the world and make their fortunes while their wives are buried alive at home—but they cannot lightly go against the will of the *halga*. A respected and enlightened Mozabite took his wife to France for a holiday; they were both banned and forbidden to re-enter the community until they paid a stiff fine. Since their enclave of Ghardaïa is on the desert "oil route" to Hassi Messaoud and Edjeleh, it is bound to enjoy increasing prosperity and ever greater contact with the present day, but any changes in the Mozabites' narrow pattern of private life will come slowly.

Within the memory of all these oddly assorted peoples, the Sahara was their own preserve, harsh and hot and bloodied at

A Home to Fit the Needs

Desert tribes build shelters that reflect their habits. The most primitive nomads, like the Bushmen and Bindibu, often have nothing more than a tuft of grass. More advanced nomads generally have tents that are easily erected, taken down and carried. In summer the Tuareg use a zeriba of grass and wood; in cooler weather, they turn to leather tents. The Bedouin tent is made of goat-hair cloth. The Mongol yurt is made of felt or fur on springy willow poles. Non-nomadic tribes tend to build permanent homes such as the Navahos' hogans of logs and mud.

NAVAHO HOGAN

MONGOL YURT

Eurasia

MONGOLIANS

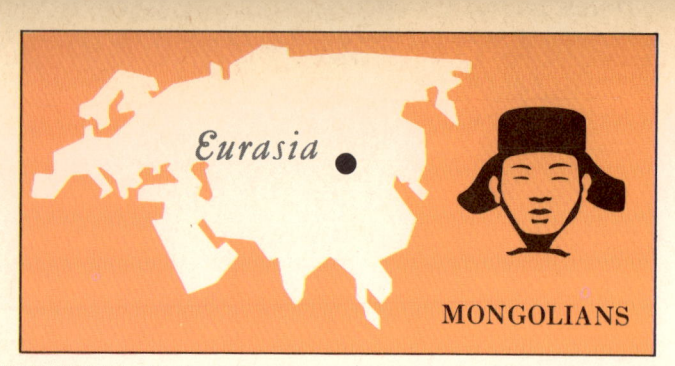

times with their conflicts, but blessedly out of sight, out of mind to the rest of the world. This is no longer true: their desert is suddenly engulfed by the mainstream of human events, suddenly of strategic, political and industrial importance, and suddenly overrun by the men of the modern world, and *their* machines, and *their* conflicts. The desert peoples have done well to survive the endless onslaught of the sun; they will be luckier to survive the merciless onslaught of the 20th Century.

108

Roaming to Find Necessities

Dwarfed by the vast steppe lands, a lone Mongolian watches his herd browse on the sparse grass. When this forage gives out, he will move his animals to other grazing areas. Many desert people are nomadic —for their lands' shifting patterns of rainfall, plant growth and animal life force them to move.

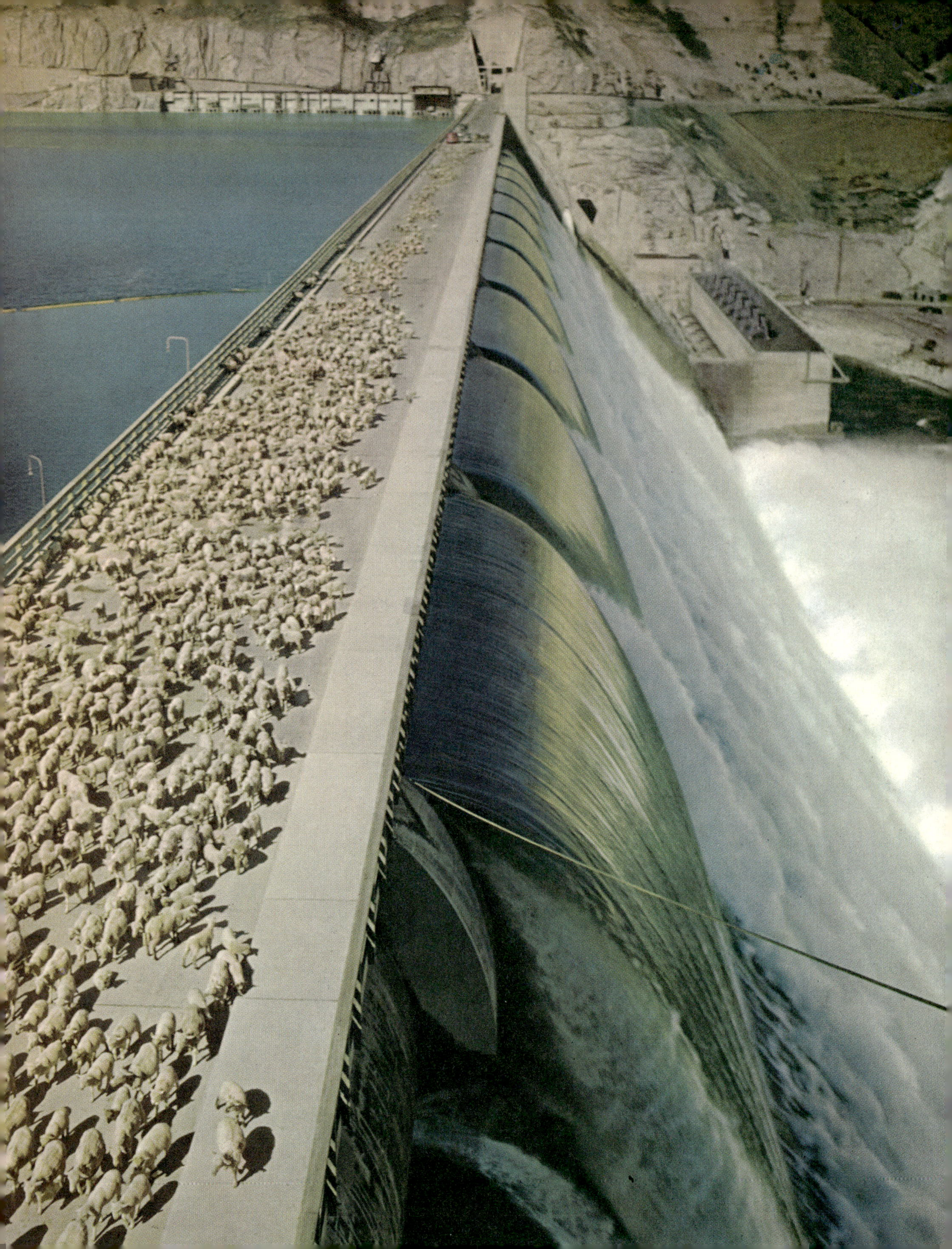

7
Taming the Desert for Mankind's Use

HUNDREDS OF SHEEP heading for green pastures jam traffic atop the Grand Coulee Dam in Washington. This dam, which harnesses the Columbia River and provides water for irrigation, has helped turn a million acres of arid land in the Pacific Northwest into important sources of food.

In the wrinkled old hills of the Holy Land south and west of the Dead Sea it rains two to four inches a year, and the roar of the rare torrents tumbling down normally dry gullies is the loudest noise the Negev highlands ever hear. Two thousand years ago, however, this was a province of the Nabataeans, an industrious, grain-growing people who tamed the waters with one of the most elaborate irrigation systems ever built.

Improving on techniques thought up at least a thousand years earlier by the Phoenicians, the Nabataeans threw across the river beds, or wadies, low dams of rocks. Each dam trapped and held a level plot of soil that became a tiny cultivated field. Retaining walls and ditches cut into the hillsides controlled the water that ran down from the hills, and dense shrubbery planted along the dams held the rocks in place and further slowed the water's descent. Cisterns carved out of rock gathered enough water for the people and their cattle, but most of the scant rainfall went to the crops. Nabataean records tell of the yields: eight measures of barley and seven of wheat for each measure of seed sown. Considering the problems, their figs, dates and grapes all did well.

Although the Nabataeans were conquered by Rome in 106 A.D., their farming system survived for another 600 years until it was destroyed around 700 by the newly powerful Muslims. For more than 12 centuries thereafter the Negev was utterly neglected. The torrents obliterated the untended irrigation works, and the sheep, goats and camels of heedless nomads grazed the land until it was bare of plants; on the stripped hills, erosion went on unchecked.

This miserable countryside, a desert if there ever was one, went to Israel in the 1948 partition of Palestine. Today it is part of an experiment closely bound up with the future of the whole Mediterranean basin and, for that matter, the future of mankind. In their wasteland the Israelis have more than doubled the extent of usable agricultural land. By developing wells and putting the limited surface waters to better use, they have irrigated 325,000 dry acres. And they are rebuilding and expanding the waterworks of the ancient Nabataean engineers.

To make sure these improvements will last, the Israelis are doing what their predecessors never did—planting grasses and forests in the uplands to protect the watersheds from erosion. Their livestock is pastured on the hills, but in numbers controlled to prevent overgrazing, the curse of so many arid lands. As a result, the Middle East's newest nation already is able to export farm produce. The control center of this great experiment, the Negev Institute for Arid Zone Research, is located in Beersheba, principal city of the Negev, which has grown from a population of 2,000 to 65,000 since 1949. Farming is not the only industry being restored in the Negev. Located by archeologists, with hints from the Bible, copper is being mined from deposits first worked in King Solomon's time. Promising oil strikes have also been made.

The mineral richness of desert soils virtually assures good crop growth when water is supplied. Irrigation, therefore, is the most dramatic way to increase production in arid lands. Some of America's most highly productive farmlands are the irrigated valleys of the Rio Grande and the Pecos Rivers in New Mexico and Texas, the Gila and Salt River Valleys in Arizona, and the San Joaquin, Sacramento and Imperial Valleys of California. The vast Colorado-Big Thompson project, which carries water under the Rockies from the snowy watersheds on the west to semiarid southeastern Colorado on the east, and the Columbia Basin project in eastern Washington are among man's boldest attempts to change the natural distribution of water for human benefit. Egypt's Aswân High Dam has drowned ancient temples and tombs along 300 miles of the Nile, but will bring two and a half million acres into bloom. The Soviet Union's plans dwarf all the others: it is damming the Don, the Volga, the Amu Darya and other rivers in order to bring water to 70 million dry acres.

Irrigation: Key to Life

One of the most impressive examples of how irrigation has reclaimed desert land is the 650,000-acre Imperial Valley (*bottom right*), in the Sonoran Desert of California. To turn the valley into valuable farmlands, engineers constructed the arrow-straight All-American Canal (*right*). Daily, it brings millions of gallons of Colorado River water to the valley, which produces crops worth more than $150 million yearly.

Desert irrigation, however, is an extremely tricky business. If the water is allowed to stand and evaporate, it leaves behind the salts it has carried in solution—salts that can kill vegetation. Moreover, standing water also draws to the surface salts which are already in the soil. To prevent this, an irrigation system must provide for the overflow from reservoirs so that the water can flow downstream where it is needed. But because such a drainage system was never installed, much of the irrigated land in Iraq is now dangerously salty. In another example, an elaborate and costly irrigation system was completed on Turkey's Menemen Plain in 1949, without provision for drainage. Much of the land it served has turned so salty that nothing will grow.

There are other drawbacks to desert irrigation. Many of the deep wells being drilled today in deserts around the world are using up water that can never be replaced. In Mexico, there are short-term farming projects in parts of Baja California and Sonora using wells that will probably run dry in only 10 to 15 years. Such use of water deposits cannot be looked upon as agricultural progress.

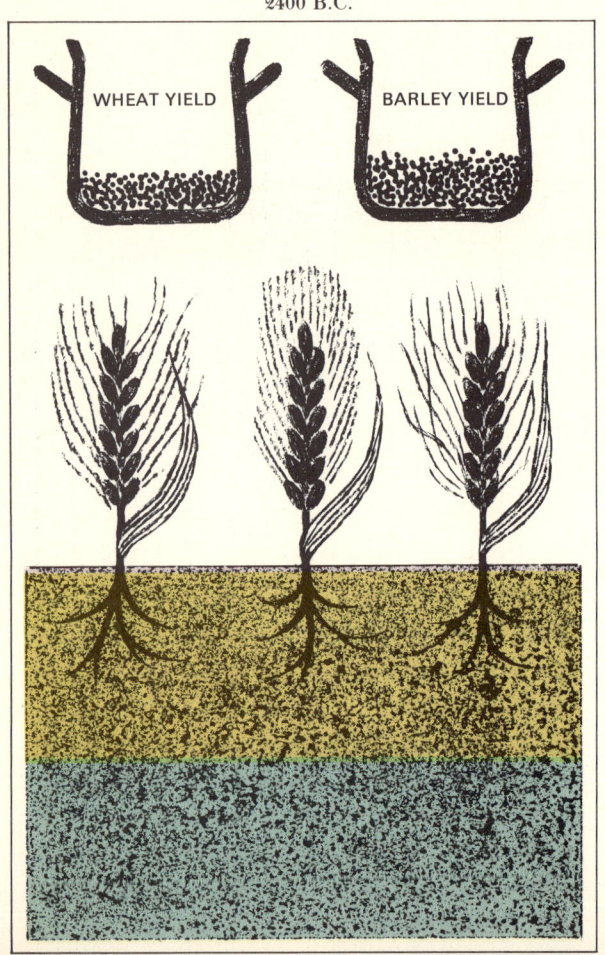

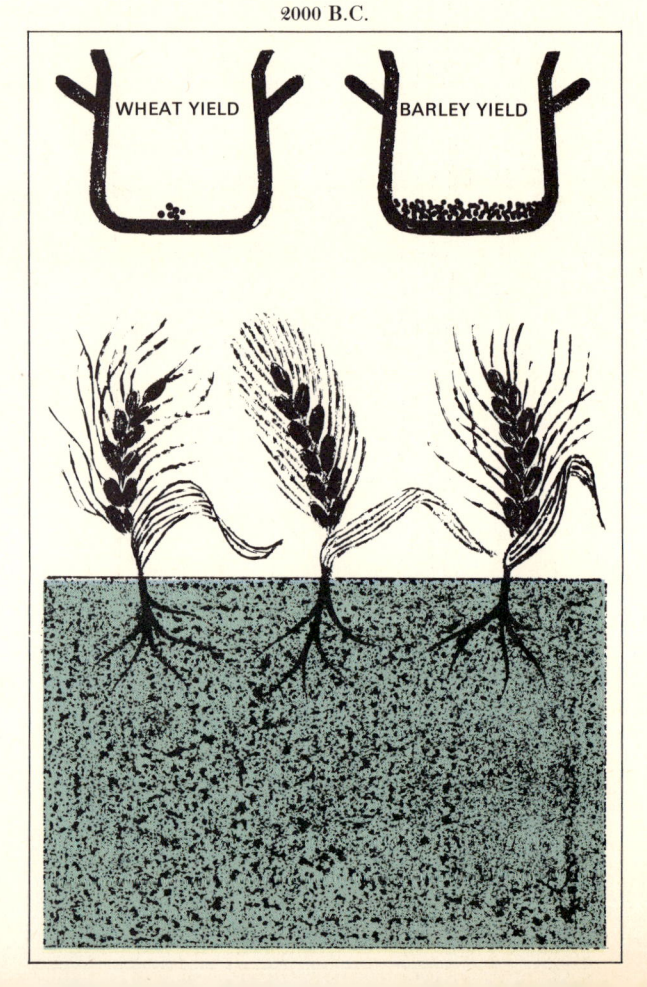

Only a small part of the desert lends itself to irrigation, but much of the rest can be grazed by livestock. However, keeping too many animals on dry land is extremely dangerous. More civilizations have collapsed because of failure to understand the disastrous effects of overgrazing on desert vegetation than have been destroyed by all other factors together—including war and pestilence.

It is difficult for man to see that he may be harming himself when he looks out on a quiet scene of cattle or goats grazing contentedly on a hillside in an area with little rainfall. For the early stages of overgrazing do not hurt the animals. An arid grassland or shrubland can continue producing fat cattle, sheep or goats long after nourishing grasses have begun to have trouble replacing what the animals eat. It is only when the grasses suddenly vanish and only useless weeds remain that farmers realize what has happened. Then it is too late.

In more humid lands, a ruined pasture can be restored fairly easily by the use of fertilizer and lime and by replanting with the seed of a desirable forage plant; the yields from the restored fields are high enough to pay the cost. But on desert lands, forage yields are uncertain and usually low; the job of restoring the soil is terribly expensive, and returns are slow in coming in. Yet in the long run the

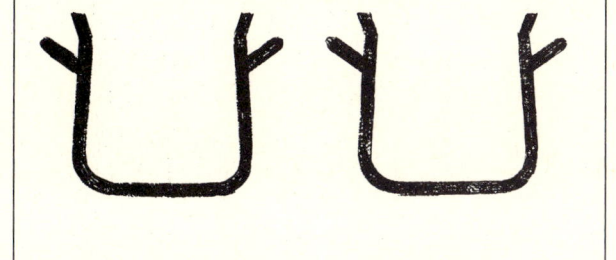

Irrigation That Backfired

These diagrams illustrate how too much water—salty water—ruined the lush lands of Mesopotamia (now Iraq). Before 2400 B.C., as heavy use of salty river water raised the level of salty, underground water, wheat still flourished but farmers were beginning to plant barley, a plant more resistant to salt. By 2000 B.C. even the barley was failing. As the land and the water table became even saltier, the topsoil was completely ruined and the area became a waterless wasteland. Now, careful irrigation is restoring the land.

FARMABLE TOPSOIL

WATER TABLE

UNFARMABLE TOPSOIL

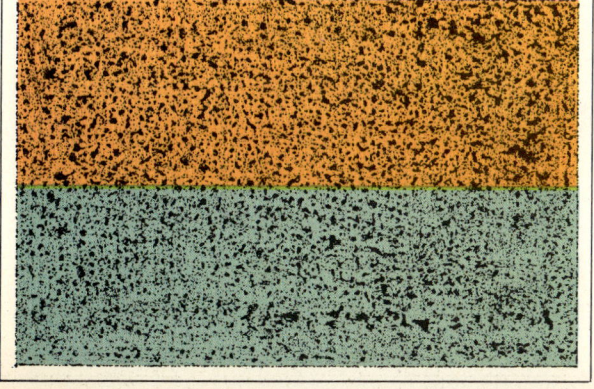

A Project to Tame the Nile

Symbol of ancient Egypt, the temple of Abu Simbel (*below*) was almost lost to the Aswân Dam, designed to reclaim two million acres of desert by irrigation. The lake formed by the Aswân would have drowned Abu Simbel, but technicians raised the temple before flooding began. The statue of Rameses II (*left*) will go to a museum to save it from flooding.

restoration of arid ranges will be of tremendous benefit to mankind. In fact a good many nations owning mostly desert or semi-desert lands will have to start such programs if they expect to feed their people.

Unfortunately, not all desert lands can be turned into stock pastures. Very large areas are too dry to grow more than an occasional crop of desert annuals, vegetation that can feed the little bands of goats owned by wandering nomads. But perhaps half of the world's deserts get enough rainfall to sustain at least light livestock grazing, and under careful range management this enormous area could contribute mightily to the world food supply.

The most obvious riches of the arid lands, and the most coveted, are the deposits of oil and valuable minerals. Many of the world's greatest oil fields—like those in Arabia and Iraq, western Texas and the southern San Joaquin Valley of California—are located in deserts. Yet, not too many years ago French government authorities were still impatiently waving aside the scientists who claimed that oil must underlie certain geologic formations in the Sahara. But the geologists were stubborn, too, and by 1961 the Saharan wells were producing about 16 million tons of oil a year; the air-conditioned boom

A Staircase Full of Copper

Rising like stadium bleachers, the terraced sides of a copper mine dwarf the digging equipment on the mine's floor. Located in Chile's Atacama Desert, this pit is the world's most productive copper mine. In 1966, some 48 million tons of ore and waste were dredged up to produce about 335,000 tons of copper.

towns of Hassi Messaoud and Edjeleh, complete with swimming pools and movie theaters, were thriving on the desert.

Also scattered about the deserts are some fabulously rich mines—silver in northern Mexico, copper in Nevada and Peru, uranium in Utah and New Mexico, diamonds in South Africa and so on. A certain class of minerals exists in the desert just because of the dryness; these chemicals, deposited by water as it evaporates, include salt, gypsum, borax, nitrates and phosphates. One of these desert minerals, borax, is so valuable that a billion dollars' worth of borax is being scooped out of the world's biggest deposit, in California's Mojave Desert, partly in order to extract a few pounds a day of boron for research on rocket fuels and new plastics.

Some of the plants that grow in deserts supply very valuable materials. In the Soviet Union, for example, a large part of its synthetic rubber is now derived from two plants of the dandelion family. First discovered in the Tien Shan Mountains of Central Asia in 1930 and 1931, these wild plants are now cultivated on farms, and the latex they produce makes Russia less dependent on rubber from other countries. Many drought-resistant pasture and range grasses have been developed from wild desert plants; so have a tremendous number of

The Desert's Richest Gift

The man laying pipeline *(left)* and the long rows of 55-gallon drums *(right)* are both part of the story of oil, the black liquid that runs our modern world. Of the 300 billion barrels of untapped oil in the world, half is beneath the deserts. To reach and transport this "black gold," men have braved the desert to dig wells as deep as two miles, stretch pipelines for more than 1,000 miles, and build towns in completely isolated areas. Now six million barrels of oil a day are being pumped from the deserts.

ornamental trees and shrubs, such as tamarisk from Arabia, genesta from Libya, and Washington palm from California. Drugs, fibers, dyes, alcoholic liquors (tequila and mescal, from the century plant) and edible fruits are part of the desert's bounty.

Most species of domesticated animals originated in the deserts and arid grasslands. Ever since he first tamed these useful beasts, man has waged war against the wild animals he finds on grazing lands, so that he could use the land to pasture cattle, goats, sheep and other domesticated animals. This war is still going on in many parts of the world. In East Africa, for example, there have recently been massive slaughters of wild game animals to make it possible to raise more cattle on the range.

The wild game, besides competing with cattle for forage, carry a blood parasite called trypanosome, harmless to wild animals, but fatal to cattle when transmitted by the tsetse fly. By killing off the game animals that harbor the parasite and burning the scrub forest where the tsetse fly lives and breeds, it has been possible to introduce far more cattle than could exist there before.

Whether this is real progress is a question. In the first place, the native herders have a poor understanding of how many cattle can graze on a range without destroying the

Material for Atomic Power

This tangle of machinery is part of a Colorado plant that concentrates uranium ore. The mineral, essential in nuclear projects, is one of the desert's greatest prizes—and the most difficult to obtain. An average of 400 pounds of uranium-bearing ore must be processed to produce one pound of uranium.

grass. As a result, great tracts of semiarid grassland have been turned into desert by the pasturing of too many cattle throughout the year. Now these lands are too poor to support either game animals or livestock.

As a matter of fact, the semiarid grasslands and shrubby "bush" of Africa would produce far more meat and hides if the wild animals were protected and used as a food resource. Africa has many different hoofed animals that make far better use of the vegetation than could a domesticated species like the cow. In 1960, experiments began in Southern Rhodesia to measure the amount of meat and hides obtainable from the game on an undeveloped tract of wild bush. These figures can then be compared with known average yields from cattle herds in adjoining country. Results of this experiment are still under study, but it begins to appear that the game will outproduce the cattle by nearly 700 per cent and at a much lower cost.

Besides being useful for its resources of minerals, oil, animals and plants, the desert is proving extremely profitable as a resort area for people. Campers, hikers, rock collectors and flower lovers clamber about the wide-open spaces. Lakes—the real ones and the ones made by dams—are covered with powerboats and water skiers. The red silt that stains the Colorado River is now held by a series of upstream dams, and from Lake Mead above Hoover Dam on down to the delta in the Gulf of California the water is clear enough for good fishing.

All this does not come free; one price of the miracle of desert irrigation is the lowering of the supply of water beneath the earth's surface. Some people are concerned about this loss; many others figure that new water will be found somehow, even if it has to be piped from the Pacific and desalted.

A matter of greater concern to outdoorsmen is the rapid disappearance of privacy and solitude, which have long been primary attractions of the arid wastelands. Growing towns and resorts bring demands for more and better roads; the roads attract more people, who demand more resorts. While it is highly desirable that the sunny playgrounds be enjoyed by large numbers of people, it does not seem necessary that all parts of the desert should be made equally easy to reach by automobile. Good principles of zoning would suggest that some desert areas be preserved in their original wilderness for the more ambitious hikers and hunters who truly wish to get away from the crowds.

As the world's population grows, so does the value and importance of every natural resource. Products of the earth that were not used or needed a century ago are being pressed into service today to meet the growing demands of people and industry. There are no longer any "waste" spaces on the earth. The arctic tundra, the ocean depths, the craggy mountains and even outer space itself are all entering man's plans for his future. The deserts are a part of the world that was used only lightly (and, in general, unskillfully) by earlier men, but this poor treatment can no longer be afforded—there are too many of us now.

In some nations where men are hungry, desert lands that once were used, spoiled and discarded are being laboriously brought back to productivity. In some newer countries where there is no immediate threat of famine the problem is less acute. Nevertheless, even there, desert resources are being put to use, one by one, to yield food, minerals, living room—all things that men want and need.

Up to now men have treated the deserts as if they made no difference. One of these days, when survival no longer can be taken for granted on a crowded, used-up earth, they may make all the difference.

Where Little Bloomed Before

New towns, such as this one in California's Mojave Desert, owe their existence to improved ways of finding and carrying water over vast distances. In a crowded world, deserts offer space. Man, using modern technology, is hard at work all over the world reclaiming these previously uninhabitable areas.

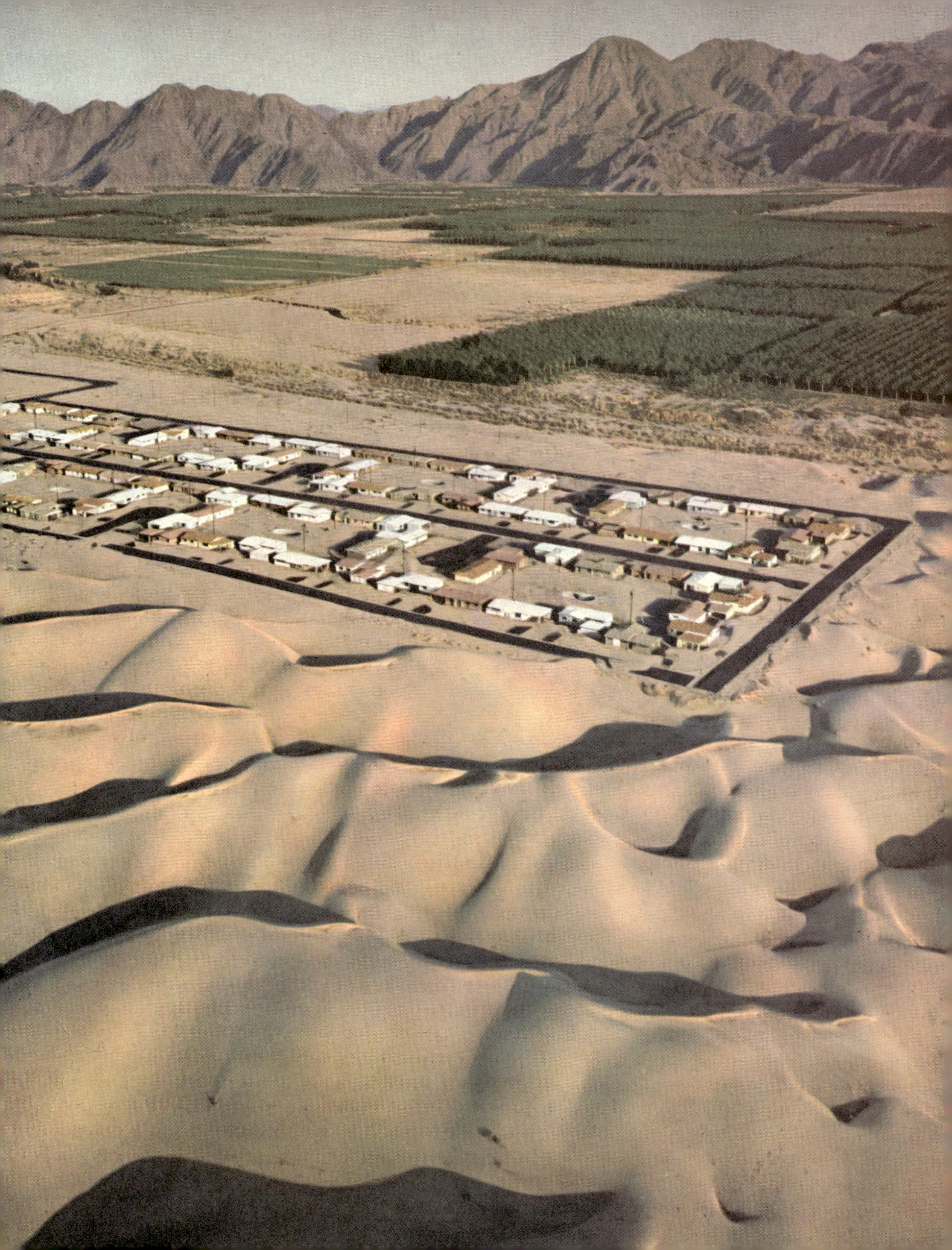

Index

Numerals in italics indicate a photograph or painting of the subject listed.

Aborigines, 86, *98-99*
Abu Simbel (temple), *116*, *117*
Acacia trees, *38-39*
Africa, 11, *38-39*, *86-87*; animals of, 121, 123. See also specific regions, e.g., Sahara; and see specific tribes
Agriculture, 17, 22-23, 101, *113*, *114-115*, 117; ancient systems of, 12, 111-112. See also Grazing lands; Irrigation
Air currents, and desert formation, 19
Alfalfa hay, 17
All-American Canal, *113*
Amphibians, 55
Ancient civilizations, 11, 12; art of, *90-91*, 101, *116*; farming systems, 12, 111-112
Animals: adaptations of, 51-68, 77, 78, *80-81*; dependence on plants, 47, 49, *70*, *73*; domestic, 99, 112, 121, 123; marsupial, 68, 72; and seed germination, 40, 68; water supply, 32, 52-53, 55, 62, 68, 71-72, 75-76, 78, 83. See also specific names, e.g., Camel
Ant, honeypot, *64-65*
Aquatic life, *52-53*, 55, *67*
Arabian Desert, 9
Arabs, *96-97*, 105-107
Arizona, 10, 11, 60, 104
Art: ancient, *90-91*, *116-117*; Indian, *102-103*
Artesian wells, 21
Arthropods, 63
Ash Meadows, Nevada, 55
Ass, *52-53*
Aswân High Dam, 112, 116
Atacama-Peruvian Desert, *8*, *12-13*
Australian Desert, 9, 45, 68; aborigines of, 86, *98-99*

Badger, *54-55*
Baja California, 11, 13, 114
Baobab tree, 40
Barkhan dunes, *14*
Barrel cactus, *36*, 38, 40, *43*
Bat, 75
Bedouin, 99, 107
Benson, Seth B., 66
Bi, tuber vine, 45
Bicycle Dry Lake, *52-53*, *67*
Bindibu, 107
Birds, 62, 64, 82. See also specific birds, e.g., Owl
Bonneville Salt Flats, *25*
Borax, 120
Borrego Desert, *34*
Brittlebush, 45
Bryce Canyon, Utah, *6-7*
Bulbs, 37, 43, 45
Burrows, *56*, 66, 71
Bushmen, *84-85*, *86-87*, *88-89*, 95, 97, 99, 101, 107
Butte, *18*, *21*, *23*

Cacti, *26*, *36*, 37, 38, 40, *41*, *42-43*, 44, *46-47*, 49, 73
California, *8*, 17, *113*, 125
Camel, *52-53*, *76-77*; trade, 101, 102
Canals, *113*
Candy cactus, *49*
Canyons, *16-17*, *18*, *20-21*, 28
Caravans, *14-15*, 95, 101
Carnivores, 64, 71, 75
Caspian Sea, 10
Cattle, 101, 121, 123; tracks of, *79*
Caucasian tribes, 86, 88
Cereus, night-blooming, 37, 45
Chamba tribe, 105-106
Chenopod, *42-43*
Chihuahuan Desert, 10-11
Chlorophyll, 42
Cholla cactus, 40
Cities, *125*; ancient, 11, 12
Clothing, 86, 88, *92-93*, *94*, 95, 99, 101
Color, and selective evolution, 66
Colorado River, *16-17*, 30, 113; Valley, 28; Big Thompson project, 112
Columbia River, 111; Basin project, 112
Copper, 112
Creosote, *34*

Dams, 21, *110*, 111, 112, 116
Dandelion, 120
Death Valley, 40
Deer, mule, 72
Defense: animal coloration, 66; of desert rats, *56-57*; of plants, 37, *44*, 45; of reptiles, 61-62, *80-81*
Dehydration, 91-92
Desalination, 20-21
Desert dwellers: adaptations of, 85-86, 88, 91-92, 95, 97, 99, 101-102, 105-108; homes of, 99, *104-105*, *106-107*; primitive art of, *90-91*. See also specific groups, e.g., Bushmen
Deserts: age of, 22; features of, 8, 13; formation of, 8, *18*, *22-23*; location of, maps 8-9, 17, 19; water distribution in, 20-21. See also specific deserts
Dew, 31-32
Dormancy: of animals, 78, 80, 82; of plants, 35. See also Estivation
Dunes, *12-13*, *14-15*; formation of, *14*, 24; and mesquite, 40
"Dust Bowl," 22
Dust storms, 24
Duvdevani, Shmuel, 31-32

Earth: desert locations, map 8-9, 17, 19; and sun's radiation, charts 10-11, 15, 17
Egypt, 112, *116-117*
Equator, maps 8-9, 17
Erosion, *6-7*, *16-17*, *18*, 22-24
Estivation, 55, 81

Evaporation. See Water
Excretion, 72, 75

Fat, of camel, 76, 77
Fish, 53, 55
Floods, flash, 23, 26, 28, 31
Food: of animals, 54, 64, 71-72, 75-76, 78, 80-82; of ants, *64-65*; and body wastes, 72, 75; cactus fruit as, *43*, *49*; of desert dwellers, 89, 95; insects as, 48, 51, 63; natural interdependence, 51; seeds as, 64, 66, 76
Fox, kit, *50*
Fruit, of cacti, 38, 40, *43*, 49

Gerbil, 66, 68
Gila monster, 60
Giraffe, *69*
Gobi Desert, 12, 19
Grand Coulee Dam, *110*
Grazing lands, 19; overgrazing, *22-23*, 78, 112, 115, 121, 123
Great Basin Desert, 10
Great Indian Desert (Thar), 11

Hedgehog cactus, *36*, 40, *43*
Homes, 99, 101, 102, *104-105*, *106-107*; cactus as, *73*
Hot springs, 31
Humboldt River, Nevada, 17
Hummingbird, 82
Hunting, 87, *88-89*, 95, 97, 98

Imperial Valley, California, 17, *113*
Indians, American, *100-101*, *104-105*; art of, *102-103*; use of cacti, 38, 40, 43
Indus River, 30; Valley, 11
Insects, 48, 52, 63, 75
Iranian Desert, 12
Iraq, 32, 115
Irrigation, 17, *20-21*, 30, *110*, 111-112, *113*, *114-115*, 124
Israel, agriculture in, 112

Jerboa, 68, *74*
Joshua tree, 42

Kalahari Desert, 9, 11-12, 40, *84-85*, *86-87*, *88-89*, 95
Kangaroo rat, *57*, 66, 68, *74*, 76
Kara Kum Desert, 66

Lakes, 13, *79*; salt, *21*. See also specific lakes
Land forms, *6-7*, *14*, *16-17*, *18*, *20-21*, *22-24*. See also Dunes
Leaves, 35, 37, *42-43*, 44

126

Libyan Desert, *12-13*
Lizard, 58-60, 66, *80-81;* gecko, *60;* and heat, 61
Longitudinal dunes, *14*

"Meharistes," 105
Menemen Plain, Turkey, 114
Mesa, *21*, 23, *104-105*
Mesquite, *37*, 40, 78
Mexico, 13
Mice, pocket, 66, 80-82
Middle East, 22, 112
Migration: of birds, 62; of desert tribes, 101
Minerals, 17, 112, 117-118, 119, 120-122
Mojave Desert, 10, 28, 53, 57, 66, 120, *125*
Mongols, 86, 99, 107, *108-109*
Morocco, 105
Mountains, *20*, 28; and desert formation, *18*, *19;* Sahara, 13
Mozabites, 106-107
Mud flats, *12*
Muslims, *96-97*, 102, 106
Mzab River, 106

Nabataeans, 111-112
Navaho Indians, 102, 107
Negev Desert, 111-112
Negroid tribes, 86-88
Neolithic man, 12
Nevada, 17, 31
Nile River, 30, *116-117*
Nomads, *84-85*, *92-93*, 95, *98-99*, 105, 107; and grazing lands, *32*, *108-109*
North America, western deserts of, *8*, 10-11, 22, 23, *100*. See also specific deserts

Oases, *21*, 30-31
Oceans, *20;* currents and desert formation, 8, 19; desalination of, 21
Ocotillo, 37, *42-43*, *44*
Oil, 112, 117-118, 121
Organ cactus, 40
Owl, elf, *73*

Pacific Ocean, 19
Pack rat, *56*, *70*
Paloverde tree, 42
Patagonian Desert, 11
Peru Current, 19
Plants: adaptations of, 8, 35, *36-37*, *38-39;* animal dependence on, 47, 49, 51, 70, 71, 73; annual, 36, 45-47; by-products of, 120-121; defense of, 37, *44*, 45; dormancy, 35; perennial, 45; protective, 19, *22-23*, *46-47;* seed germination of, 40, 42, 46-48; water supply of, 32, 35, 36-37, 38, 40, *41*, 43; See also specific names, e.g., Cacti

Poison: of brittlebush, 45; of Gila monster, 60
Poorwill, 66, 82
Potash, 17
Prickly pear, *36*, *44*, *70*
Primrose, *37*
Pueblo Indians, adobe homes of, 101, *104-105*
Puncture vine, *44*
Pupfish, 55

Rabbit, 72, 78; tracks of, *79*
Racer, snake, *61*
Rainfall, 8-9, 11-13, 15, 17, 19, 22-23, *26*, 27-28, 35; annual, in three areas, *chart* 28; and bird nesting, 62; phantom rain, *32-33*. See also Water
Ramses II, statue, *117*
Rattlesnake, and heat, *61*
Religion, 96, 106-107
Reproduction: of amphibians, 55, 57; of birds, 62; of reptiles, 57
Reptiles, adaptation of, *60-61*. See also Lizards; Snakes
Requibat tribes, 102, 105
Resorts, 123, 124
Reynolds, Hudson, 66
Rivers, 28, 30. See also Dams; specific rivers
Roadrunner, 54, *58-59*, 62
Rock formations, *6-7*. See also Land forms
Rodents, 64, 66, 68, 75; as food, 54, 57, 71
Roots, plant adaptations, *36-37*, 38, 40, 41, 43, 45
Rubber, 120

Saguaro, *36*, 37, 38, *41*, *42*, *44*, 73
Sahara, 9, 13, 15, 19, *32-33*, 92, 101, 105, 107; oil in, 118, 120; size, 8; Street of Palms, 31
Salt, 114, 115; flats, 17, *21*, *25*
Sand: as erosion tool, 23-24; storms, 24. See also Dunes
Sand viper, 61
Scorpion, *63*
Sedimentary rock, 16
Seeds: of annuals, 45-48; as food, 64, 66, 75, 76, 80; germination of, 40, 42, 46-48; of mesquite, 40
Selective evolution, and coloration, 66
Shaw, W. T., 66
Sheep, *94*, *110*
Shreve, Forrest, 47
Shrimp, 53, *67*
Sierra Madre Occidental, 11
Sierra Nevada-Cascade Mountains, 10, 19
Smoke tree, 40
Snakes: adaptations of, 60-62; sense of smell, 62
Snow fields, *20*
Soil: minerals in, 17, 112, 117-118, 120; reclamation of, 20-21, 111-112, 114-115,
117; salt in, 114
Sonoran Desert, 10-11, 57, *113*
Spider, *63*
Star dunes, *14*
Succulents, 37, 45. See also Cacti
Sun, and desert radiation, *charts* 10-11, 15
Sweat glands; cooling system of animals, 59-60, 72; human rate, 88
Swift, 82

Tadpole, 57
Takla Makan Desert, 12
Teda, 102
Temperature, 31; animal endurance, 59, 71-72, 78, 80; and birds, 62, 72, 82; highest, 15; man's endurance, 85-86, 88, 91, 92, 95; and reptiles, 61, 72; and seed germination, 48; sun's radiation, *charts* 10-11, 15, 17
Thar Desert, 11
Thistle, *44*
Thomas, Elizabeth Marshall, 95
Thorns, 37, *43*, *44*, 45, *49*
Toad, spadefoot, 55
Tortoise, 57-58, *83*
Trade, nomadic, 99, 101, 102, 106
Transverse dunes, *14*
Trees, 37, *38-39*, 40, 42, 45
Tropic of Cancer, *map* 8-9, 17
Tropic of Capricorn, *map* 8-9, 17
Tuareg, *92-93*, 101-102, 107
Tubers, 43, 45
Turkistan, 9-10

Union of Soviet Socialist Republics, 112, 120
United Nations, 32
Uranium ore, 122
Utah, *6-7*, 10, *16-17*, *25*

Verbena, *34*
Vulture, 64

Wallaby, 72
Water: animal need of, 53, 71-72, 75-76, 78, 82, 83; bird need of, 62; camel storage of, 76, *77;* desert sources, 30-32; erosion caused by, *6-7*, *16-17*, *18*, *22-23;* evaporation, 12, 24, 27-28, 30; human need of, 85, 88, 91-92, 95; plant need of, 35-38, 40, 41, 43, 73; redistribution of, *20-21;* underground, 21, 28, 30, 31, 37. See also Dew; Irrigation; Rainfall
Wells, 21, 32, 114
Went, Frits, 48
Wind: and desert formation, 8, 29, 22; and dune formations, *12-13;* erosion caused by, *6-7*, 23-24
Woodpecker, Gila, 73

127

For Further Reading

Ault, Phil, *This Is the Desert*. Dodd, 1959.
Baldwin, Gordon C., *The Ancient Ones*. Norton, 1963.
Cottrell, Leonard, *The Lost Pharaohs*. Holt, 1961.
Epstein, Sam and Beryl, *All About the Desert*. Random, 1957.
Fenton, Carroll Lane and Evelyn Carswell, *Wild Folk in the Desert*. Day, 1958.
Fenton, Carroll Lane and Alice Epstein, *Cliff Dwellers of Walnut Canyon*. Day, 1960.
Goetz, Delia, *Deserts*. Morrow, 1956.
Hagaman, Adaline P., *What Is Water?* Benefic, 1960.
Huntington, Harriet E., *Let's Go to the Desert*. Doubleday, 1949.
Jaeger, Edmund C., *North American Deserts*. Stanford, 1957.
Krutch, Joseph Wood, *The Voice of the Desert: A Naturalist's Interpretation*. Sloane, 1955.
Leopold, A. Starker and the Editors of TIME-LIFE BOOKS, *The Desert*. Time Inc., 1961.
Louvain, Robert and the Staff of the Walt Disney Studio, *Wildlife of the West*. Golden, 1958.
Sears, Paul B., *Deserts on the March* (rev. ed.). University of Oklahoma, 1959.
Shannon, Terry, *Desert Dwellers*. Whitman, 1958.
Werner, Jane and the Staff of the Walt Disney Studio, *Living Desert*. Golden, 1958.

Credits

The sources for the illustrations that appear in this book are shown below. Credits for the pictures from left to right are separated by commas, top to bottom by dashes.

Cover—Horace Bristol
Table of Contents—Matt Greene—Adolph E. Brotman—Wayne Trimm—Guy Coheleach—Kenneth Gosner of the Newark Museum—Tony Saris—Otto van Eersel
6, 7—Eliot Elisofon
8, 9—Matt Greene
10, 11—Adolph E. Brotman
12, 13—Myron Davis, Aero Service Corporation
14, 15—Drawings by Adolph E. Brotman, photograph by James Burke courtesy American Museum of Natural History
16, 17—John G. Zimmerman for SPORTS ILLUSTRATED
18—Matt Greene
20, 21—Painting by Mel Hunter
22, 23—Matt Greene
25—Fritz Goro
26—Loomis Dean
28—Adolph E. Brotman
29—Loomis Dean
31—Loomis Dean
32, 33—Emil Schulthess from Black Star
34—Andreas Feininger
36, 37—Wayne Trimm
38, 39—Eliot Elisofon
41—Kenneth Gosner of the Newark Museum
42, 43—Western Ways from Photo Researchers, Inc., Arabian American Oil Co., Andreas Feininger—Western Ways from Photo Researchers, Inc.
44—Kenneth Gosner of the Newark Museum
46, 47—Dmitri Kessel
49—Loomis Dean
50—Loomis Dean
52, 53—James Burke—Emil Schulthess from Black Star
54, 55—Loomis Dean
56, 57—Loomis Dean, Guy Tudor
58, 59—Guy Coheleach
60, 61—Loomis Dean, Guy Tudor
63—Rudolf Freund (2)—Jack J. Kunz
64, 65—Dr. Thomas Eisner, René Martin
67—Loomis Dean
69—Loomis Dean
70—Loomis Dean
73—Lewis Wayne Walker courtesy Arizona-Sonora Desert Museum
74, 75—Loomis Dean—Guy Tudor
76, 77—Standard Oil Co. (New Jersey), Kenneth Gosner of the Newark Museum
78, 79—Kenneth Gosner of the Newark Museum, William A. Garnett
80, 81—Loomis Dean
83—Loomis Dean
84, 85—N. R. Farbman
86—Drawing by Otto van Eersel—N. R. Farbman
87—N. R. Farbman, Constance Stuart from Black Star
88, 89—N. R. Farbman
90, 91—Adolph E. Brotman
92, 93—Drawing by Otto van Eersel—David Douglas Duncan
94—Drawing by Otto van Eersel—David Douglas Duncan
96, 97—Drawing by Otto van Eersel—David Douglas Duncan
98, 99—Drawing by Otto van Eersel—K. Meyers, Dr. Donald Thomson
100—Drawing by Otto van Eersel—Peter Stackpole
102—Eliot Elisofon
103—Eliot Elisofon from the collections in the Museum of New Mexico
104, 105—Tony Saris—Peter Stackpole
106, 107—Tony Saris
108, 109—Drawing by Otto van Eersel—James Burke
110—Parris Emery
113—Dmitri Kessel—Otto Hagel
114, 115—Otto van Eersel
116, 117—James Burke
118, 119—Eliot Elisofon
120, 121—David Douglas Duncan
122, 123—Ezra Stoller courtesy Union Carbide Co.
125—Ralph Crane
End papers—Virginia Wells

Acknowledgments

The editors are indebted to the staff of the Life Nature Library, from which this volume is adapted; the staff for this edition: Stanley Fillmore, editor; Eric Gluckman, designer; Marianna P. Kastner and Tony Chiu, writers; Eleanor Feltser, Susan Marcus and Theo Pascal, researchers; Eleanore W. Karsten, copyreader; Virginia Wells, art assistant.